COUNTRY VET

Thirty Years of Treating Animals and
Trying to Understand Their Owners

Randy L. Skaggs, DVM

Black Rose Writing | Texas

©2022 by Randy L. Skaggs, DVM
All rights reserved. No part of this book may be reproduced, stored in a retrieval system or transmitted in any form or by any means without the prior written permission of the publishers, except by a reviewer who may quote brief passages in a review to be printed in a newspaper, magazine or journal.

The author grants the final approval for this literary material.

First printing

This is a work of fiction. Names, characters, businesses, places, events, and incidents are either the products of the author's imagination or used in a fictitious manner. Any resemblance to actual persons, living or dead, or actual events is purely coincidental.

ISBN: 978-1-68513-019-0
PUBLISHED BY BLACK ROSE WRITING
www.blackrosewriting.com

Printed in the United States of America
Suggested Retail Price (SRP) $19.95

Country Vet is printed in Bookerly

*As a planet-friendly publisher, Black Rose Writing does its best to eliminate unnecessary waste to reduce paper usage and energy costs, while never compromising the reading experience. As a result, the final word count vs. page count may not meet common expectations.

Acknowledgement

I dedicate this book to my loving wife, Cami, and wonderful family, my cherished patients and their parents, and my outstanding staff over the last thirty years. A special thank you to John R. Erickson for his valuable guidance and to Scott Cummins for making the stories come to life with illustrations.

COUNTRY VET

Foreword

Randy Skaggs and I got acquainted the way most ranchers and veterinarians get acquainted, through ranch mutts that have been snakebit, porcupined, or need booster-shot protection against rabid skunks. For years, I didn't realize that we had something in common besides dogs that ran up vet bills. I was a writer and so was he.

When he started writing a column for the local paper, I enjoyed reading his stories about kids who had graduated from Perryton High School, where had they gone after leaving town and what they were doing. He wrote well. I particularly enjoyed a two-part story he did about a friend and sent him a note, congratulating him on his good work.

This provoked an exchange of emails and at some point, he revealed he had been writing for years stories about things that happened in his veterinary practice. He had written them mostly for the amusement of his wife and daughters, hundreds of them, and had given some thought to putting them together in a book.

I don't often get involved in other peoples' books, but I had a feeling his stories would be good…and *funny*. At that time, we were in the depths of the COVID lockdown, avoiding contact with other human beings and trying to understand those we encountered who were talking through a surgical mask. Those were dark times, all the news was bad, and the world sure needed some funny stories about dogs, cats, cattle, horses, and monkeys.

He sent me a bundle of stories and I gave them an editorial haircut, which consisted mostly of shortening paragraphs and deleting details that got in the way of the storytelling. I suggested that he organize the book by subject, including a section on animals and their people.

I hadn't thought of this before, but vets have a kind of double vision on the human experience. They see us as the clients who bring in the patients and pay the bill, but they also see our sins, flaws, and weirdness reflected in our animals. Dr. Skaggs recognized early on that this was a rich source of humor—not ridicule, not humor that cuts, but the kind of organic humor that allows us to laugh at ourselves.

As I write this in September 2021, COVID cases are rising again, but Dr. Skaggs doesn't require masks in his literary vet clinic. Put your mask in a drawer and feel free to laugh all you want about dogs, cats, horses, cattle, and monkeys... and their people.

–John R. Erickson, Perryton, Texas

Preface

Being a veterinarian in a small, isolated country town in the Northeast Texas Panhandle for over thirty years has been an enjoyable experience. The area is the perfect backdrop to raise a family and practice veterinary medicine. The constant barrage of interesting cases keeps you moving and on your toes.

Perryton is a proud town of about 8,500 people, which has a strong dependency on oil production and agriculture. Many nationalities are represented in our stretch of heaven, but strong German and Spanish influences are dominant. People in the area are independent, set in their ways and strong-willed.

The weather is an angry mess in Perryton. The only constant is the wind, which howls. Winters are cold, blustery, and filled with snow. Summers are hot and dry with extended droughts. Springs are windy and packed with dangerous thunderstorms and tornadoes. Falls are the best time of the year with a mixture of all the above. As the saying goes,

"If you don't like the Panhandle weather, stick around for a few hours and it will change."

Farms and ranches in the Panhandle of Texas are large and stretch for miles, which creates a great deal of travel time to clear your mind. The land is flat and expansive. You can see for miles. No tall buildings and few trees are around to spoil your view.

The roughness of the directions to your destination is only slightly less rough than the country roads traveled to get there. Farmers use directions such as "turn at the road with the second deepest gully."

Sunsets at the end of host summer days are truly amazing in the Panhandle and signal the coming of a cool, rejuvenating night. Nighttime skies are endless. Every part of the galaxy can be seen on some nights. Other nights, it's as dark as coal.

All kinds of critters keep me busy. Just like veterinarians of old, current country vets treat anything that isn't human. There are no specialists here. The day's patients may include varieties such as a one-ounce Newt and a 2000-pound bull. Regardless of the patient, the days are filled with excitement and lead to good stories.

Introduction

For as long as I can remember, I have loved animals and at an early age; I made it my mission to become an animal doctor.

I grew up in Pampa, Texas, the son of two schoolteachers who often struggled to make ends meet while raising three kids. Animals of all sizes and shapes, show animals, horses, livestock and pets, were our constant companions.

Soon after graduating from veterinary school at Texas A&M, my wife and I moved to rural Perryton, Texas, to make our mark on the world. My goal was to make every dog's tail wag, every kitten purr, and every horse and cow buck and play in the fields.

I didn't think of myself as a writer, but with the encouragement of my family, I began writing my experiences at the office and in the field and have been doing it for thirty years. Hundreds of stories have made it to my computer and hundreds more reside on napkins, paper towels and notepaper in the bottom drawer of my desk.

This book is my first effort to share them with a wider audience. As the title suggests, I've been a "country vet," so my practice hasn't been specialized or limited to dogs, cats, birds, exotic animals, or livestock. Our clinic takes whatever patients walk in the door and we never know what that might include. The work can be messy, is often loud, and is sometimes dangerous.

Another result of being a country vet is that I can't avoid getting involved with the humans who bring me the patients, thus the book's subtitle: "Thirty Years of Treating Animals and *Trying to Understand Their Owners*." Sometimes the second part has been more of a challenge than the first, and it wasn't something we studied in our course work at vet school.

Dogs, cat, and horses are fairly predictable. Human beings can be... well, the Bible and Shakespeare's plays have attempted to explain us to us. My stories will add a few insights into human behavior from the perspective of a country vet. I've tried to see the humor in it when possible.

Living these stories and writing them down has been a lot of fun for me. I hope you enjoy them too.

Part One:
Exotic Animals

Monkey Business

Life in a veterinary clinic is filled with unpredictability. I might treat a 2000-pound bull in one appointment and a 4-ounce hedgehog with the next. The constant change from one minute to the next and the wide variety of challenges keep my mind racing and always test my skills. That's what I love about my job.

The behavior of my patients is also unpredictable and dramatically different. Even the most docile puppy can turn into Kujo without notice. The potential for the rapid development of a volatile situation is constantly present. You would think that the potential for disaster is much greater while working with a large bull. Large animals often turn dicey on a dime, but protective devices are usually in place to minimize the potential damage. I've had more than a few dicey experiences with small animals and pocket pets. And monkeys.

While Perryton, Texas, is not the exotic animal capital of the world, I still see several exotic animals, including monkeys, every year. This was especially the case when a national wind farm company brought their employees to erect several hundred large windmills in the area. Many of these folks traveled with exotic animals.

Mrs. Tinkerson worked for the wind farm and had more than her fair share of exotic animals. She and her husband lived in a small travel trailer with three parrots, two large dogs, two monkeys and a cat. It relieved her to find a vet in the middle of nowhere that could treat her capuchin monkeys. Her two monkeys were blood-related but had totally different personalities.

The first monkey she brought in was named Joey, the cutest little dude you ever saw. Joey was ten pounds of awesome. He was struggling with a nasty upper respiratory infection and allergies. He was shy and clung to his parents like a baby. Each time I attempted to listen to him with the stethoscope, he'd scream, grab the stethoscope with his foot and shove it back at me while burying his face in his dad's chest. He kept me at bay with his long tail and back feet while holding to his dad with a death grip with his hands.

I had a secret weapon up my sleeve to ease Joey's apprehension. He relaxed quickly when I offered him a few licks of a cherry sucker. He gave the sucker his full attention, which allowed me to have a quick look and listen. I returned to his bad side after giving him an injection for his allergies and infection. He threw the sucker at me in disgust. I was happy because at least it wasn't poop. A second sucker got me back in his good graces as he left.

I passed the initial test with Mrs. Tinkerson's first monkey. He survived, and I appeared to have at least a working knowledge of how to treat a monkey in her eyes. As a result, I got a chance to treat her other monkey and get my booty kicked a few weeks later.

Windmill construction crews go to work early in the morning well before sunrise. They have to get their work done before the high-powered Texas Panhandle winds kick up with the blistering sun. The start times for their workdays are very early as I had to meet Mrs. Tinkerson at the office at 6 am before she went to work.

There were several signs to warn me when she showed up at the office that this little beast wasn't sweet like Joey. Unlike Joey, Kalin arrived in a dog carrier with double zip ties, locking every potential cage opening. That should have been my first clue that something was up.

My second clue was the reason for the visit. Kalin had a bad attitude and needed an attitude adjustment. He was originally owned by Mrs. Tinkerson's late sister and seemed very happy there. Mrs. Tinkerson laughed as she remembered her sister's bad attitude and commented on how it matched Kalin's.

"They got along so well because they were both a pain in the ass!" she quipped.

After her sister's passing, Mrs. Tinkerson sold the monkey to a family on the east coast to pay for her sibling's funeral. Kalin was not well received in his new house. He sported a bad attitude and outwore his welcome. Despite not having a tooth in his head, he liked to bite. According to the story I was told, his teeth had been pulled long ago because of his aggressive tendencies.

Despite these negative warning signs, Kalin looked precious in his cage. Mrs. Tinkerson dropped him off with a warning, "Do not let go of the leash that is tied around his waist or he will be gone in a flash."

I assured her that all would be well and for her not to worry. She chuckled a "just wait and see" laugh as she left the office with the phrase, "Well anyway, good luck!"

My third clue about potential issues was that Kalin showed no sign of fear as I peered into the cage. He glared at me with a look of disdain. When I got near, he tried to grab me by reaching through the cage door openings with his cute little digits. He also talked "smack" to me from inside the cage. He chattered constantly and threw his head from side to side with an attitude for emphasis.

Nonetheless, I felt I was up for the battle. I closed the doors to the exam room, triple checked the dose of the medication that I planned to give, drew up the dose and psyched myself up. I gave no thought to waiting two hours for re-enforcements to arrive. This was a big mistake. I thought I could certainly handle this task. Besides, it would be better to get this done before the noise of the hectic day started and before Kalin got stirred up.

After checking the exam room doors and the anesthetic doses once again, I cut the zip ties off the carrier door. I secured the leash around my arm, opened the door, and coaxed him out. I used the usual voice that I rely on when talking to animals. It resembles baby talk.

I clapped my hands together and said, "Come here, you cute little monkey, monkey, monkey. You're a cute little monkey wonkey, come here monkey, wonkey!"

Come here, he did. Kalin sprang out of the cage, ran up my arm, grabbed me from behind my head, and choked me with his tail and legs. I gasped for air while trying to break free of his sleeper hold. It happened so fast that I was totally stunned.

I didn't gasp for long as Kalin went on the offensive and tried to get me in an arm bar hold. He swung around my neck, grabbed the collar of my shirt with his front legs and kicked me in my big belly by jumping up and down with his hind legs. All the while, Kalin was screaming like it was the Wild Kingdom Show. He definitely appeared to be enjoying himself.

I absorbed several blows to my midsection before he refocused his assault. He let go of my collar with his right hand, punched me in the cheek, scratched my nose and face, pulled my glasses off, slung them across the room, and glared at me with a defiant look. I didn't know what to do.

I reached to grab him, only to be bitten numerous times with slobbering monkey gums. Although he was toothless, his bites hurt like the dickens. I screamed in pain like I was on the Wild Kingdom Show. I definitely appeared to not be enjoying myself. Kalin was like a nimble little martial artist. I couldn't get a grip on him.

The carnage continued for several minutes, with several unsuccessful attempts by me to bring him into submission. He had a countermove for each of my offensive maneuvers. By blind luck, I discovered my secret weapon. He had no answer for my big old belly. I used my big belly as a weapon. I laid on him and held him down on the table with it. This freed up one of my arms, which allowed me to grab the anesthetic.

I gave the injection of Valium and Ketamine somewhere in the monkey's backside. The medication burned severely, which turned up his aggressive nature another notch. I held tightly and continued to lie on top of him for the next several minutes until the anesthetic kicked in.

After what seemed like an eternity, Kalin went from talking monkey smack to snoring loudly. I surveyed my wounds briefly and repaired my glasses before going to work.

Despite living through a thorough booty-pounding and sustaining severe emotional trauma, I got the last laugh. I castrated Kalin.

Hopefully, this would take away some of his aggression and prevent him from masturbating anytime company arrived. Of course, I closed his incision with sutures that would dissolve because I sure didn't want to go through another round in the octagon with him.

Even though the surgery went by without a hitch, the replacement of his diaper was a disaster. I struggled for several minutes, trying to figure out where his tail exited the diaper. I never figured it out. I stuffed it through one of the leg holes when he began to grumble as the anesthetic was wearing off.

Next, I took a few selfies with the monkey. To this day, those are the only selfies that I've ever taken. I enjoy looking back on them and showing them off when I tell the story. Despite Kalin being sound asleep, one of these photos looks exactly like a mug shot. He appears to have a nasty, death-inferring glare on his face.

As the day progressed, Kalin and I made up. I fed him the treats that Mrs. Tinkerson had left and the tension between us seemed to melt away. She left an array of treats, including monkey cakes, green grapes and orange Jello squares. He really did not like the monkey cakes. Kalin grabbed them from my hand and threw them down in disgust. He ate them only when all the other treats were gone.

He loved the juicy grapes. Actually, he just loved the inside of the grapes. He spit the skins out and only ingested those after enjoying the juicy center. When all the rest of the grape was gone, he scooped up the skins and gobbled them down while making the sour face of an old cowboy without teeth.

While the grapes helped, the food that really allowed us to bond was the orange Jello squares. He slurped the Jello like a little kid and gummed it thoroughly to savor that orange flavor. It was a lot of fun to watch.

The Jello brought delight to both of us.

I briefly considered offering him one of my suckers, since we were getting along so well. I could not do it because I was afraid of what body cavity of mine that he might shove it in. I was not going to provide him with any potential weapon that could be turned into a shank. After being manhandled by the precious little monkey earlier in the day, I wasn't taking any more chances.

For several days, I had facial wounds and couldn't bend my index fingers because of the pain and swelling from his bites. Even without teeth, Kalin could do a great deal of damage with a few gum bites. My fingers resembled polish sausages.

As I reflect on it now, I'm just glad that the tide turned, and things started going my way. If not, Kalin might have been the one grabbing the anesthetic shot and I might be the one neutered and wearing a misplaced diaper.

Making Mad Pharmacological Love

On a blistery snowy January day, the Game Warden called at closing time to ask if I would stay a few minutes late to work on a poisoned Bald Eagle. He had traveled about 45 miles to get the bird and was having a difficult time traveling back because of the terrible road conditions. They had found the eagle in a wheat field next to some dead coyotes, which he had been feasting on.

The Game Warden presumed the coyotes had been poisoned. Since January is in the calving season and coyotes are starving in the dead of winter, they create a big problem for ranchers and their new baby calves. The coyotes will attack the newborn calves or even the mother while she is trying to deliver the calf. It is common for ranchers to set traps and apply poisons to meat scraps, hoping to decrease their coyote population and their cattle losses.

The FDA and USDA have shortened the list of available poisons to use on wildlife pests, but many farmers have been harboring their old, outlawed favorites for years. Since the use of these old poisons is illegal, it is impossible to get anyone to admit which poison they are using or even claim responsibility for placing the poison.

When the eagle arrived at the clinic, it was very cold and unable to stand or even hold its head up. Since there are only about 3800 pairs of Bald Eagles in the United States, it is not common to see them in the flat, treeless Texas Panhandle. This was the first one I had seen up close.

The bird was magnificent, even in its ill state. It was a young adult male, and the Game Warden had seen its mate flying in the area near where he was found. He was old enough to have the white feathers on his head, which gave him the bald look from a distance. His wingspan was very impressive and was as long as my out-stretched arms.

The bird's beak and claws were razor sharp and intimidating. Even though he could not get up, I was very careful in getting him out of the cage and stayed clear of his claws and beak. His body had generalized muscle tremors and convulsions and his eyelids were rhythmically blinking.

Poisonous medications can be placed into a few different categories that have the same mechanisms of action and clinical signs. Many poisons have a specific antidote that can reverse the effects of the poison quickly and sometimes even instantaneously. Unfortunately, this Bald Eagle's clinical signs did not indicate one particular poison or disease.

Faced with this problem, I recalled the advice of a wise, old instructor in vet school who passed on this pearl of wisdom to me. "When in doubt of a specific diagnosis, make mad, passionate pharmacological love to them by giving every drug which you think may help".

This pearl has served me well throughout my veterinary career. I broke out the toxicology textbook and began administering every antidote that I had, and that would not complicate matters. I used only the antidotes that would not cause any harm or make the bird sicker. My gut feeling was a cyanide toxicity, but I could not be sure, and time was critical.

Besides the antidotes, I gave antibiotics for a potential meningitis and fluids with dextrose to warm his body and give him energy. We warmed his body with hot water bottles and hot towels out of the dryer. Lastly, I followed the advice of my first boss and mentor, Dr. Ron Easley, "Nothing deserves to die without the benefits of cortisone."

After giving the cortisone, I knew I had thrown everything but the kitchen sink at him and he would either make it or not. On the way to the warm isolation cage, I had my technician take my picture holding the bird, so I could prove his existence when telling this story in the future.

I started to place the bird on my shoulder like a parrot for the picture. I stopped for fear that the antidotes would kick in and the bird would quickly awaken and tear my ear off with his sharp claws. Instead, I opted for holding him at arms-length and wearing my usual goofy grin.

Throughout the night, the bird lay motionless in the cage, but slowly became more alert and responsive. The next morning, the magnificent bird was standing and ready to eat. He was tired and weak, but much improved. The Game Warden searched all the next day to find roadkill that the bird could eat but was unsuccessful.

We had to resort to chicken gizzards and livers from the grocery store that had been warmed to body temperature in the microwave. The Warden even tried to shoot a duck since it was duck hunting season, but his gun "jammed" and he missed. I think he was like me and couldn't bring himself to kill another animal just to feed the bird, even if it was our national symbol.

Thank goodness the eagle wasn't a picky eater and thrived on the chicken gizzards and livers. Most wild animals do poorly in hospital confinement, so we were eager to get the eagle strong enough to be released. That time could not come fast enough. The paperwork is substantial when rehabilitating an endangered national treasure, and I sure did not want him to die on my watch.

All eagles that die are the property of various Indian tribes and have to be sent to their headquarters. They then use the bird's feathers in ceremonial clothing and other tribe functions.

I kept the bird for four days while he got his strength back. I showed him off to anyone who came into the clinic and was brave enough to peek through the isolation door. The eagle was an unusual bird and seemed to sense that we were trying to help him. He never fought or attacked us as we cleaned his cage and fed him daily. He even ingested the gizzards that contained the bitter medication without objection.

The day we released him was a very nice day for the middle of winter. The plan was to clean up the dead coyotes and release him in the same area he was found so he could reunite with his mate. Getting the eagle back in the carrier to be transported was a real challenge. While he didn't mind the other intrusions, he was not fond of the idea of being pushed into the carrier.

As usual, the Game Warden who was trained and supposedly well equipped for such emergencies, had no equipment and stood outside the isolation room until I had him securely in the cage. We did not know if the bird could fly because our facilities would not allow him to fly well. The Game Warden asked to borrow a beach towel to catch the bird in case he could not fly.

The public should lobby for the government to issue Bald Eagle capturing beach towels to each warden since they are our national bird. The towels would probably cost the government about $1759.00 each.

The eagle release was remarkable as the beautiful bird flew to the sky and soared overhead. It is easy to see why our country's founding fathers named this wonderful specimen as our national bird. No medal or accommodation could equal my feeling of pride in seeing this beautiful bird soar in the sky and reunite with his mate.

Adequately Equipped and Well Trained

Late in the afternoon on a cool fall day, the local Animal Control Officer pulled into my driveway, going fast and furious. A call from an excited police officer had interrupted his afternoon of lounging and watching football. She was investigating a report by a small boy that he was attacked by a large, unusual animal as he opened the lid to his trash dumpster.

The animal apparently was surprised by the boy and jumped out to bite the boy's face in defense. The bite required several stitches and a tetanus injection. Finding and quarantining the animal was necessary to prevent the poor child from going through the painful Rabies vaccination series. We searched all the area dumpsters and backyards for the unidentified culprit.

All investigators had to go on was the creature was agile, aggressive and larger than a raccoon. Thanks to an exhaustive search by the police officer, the large, sharp-toothed animal had been cornered in a backyard. They then summoned the Animal Control Officer to help secure the oversized raccoon-like animal. Amazingly, they could coax the animal into a trap cage with food and bring it to my house.

John had been the Animal Control Officer for several years. He had a big, soft heart to match his big, soft frame. He was about six foot four inches and three hundred pounds. John smoked like a chimney and seemed quite ruffled most of the time. John rarely got in a hurry and seldom made many stray animal pickups because he didn't want to feed and care for them at the shelter.

He kept his equipment in terrible condition, with everything in disarray. This day he was in a big hurry and things were flying out of his truck as he sped into my drive and came to a screeching halt. Clothes, papers and other trash hit the pavement as John jumped out of the truck and yelled, "I've got a good one for you this time, Doc!".

I figured it must be exciting because I had never seen John move so quickly. I showed less excitement because living in a small town gave me many opportunities to be greeted at my front door by excited Good Samaritans with stray or injured animals. I really needed to finish mowing my knee-high lawn before I would be forced to bale it.

Reluctantly, I turned the mower off and checked the animal more closely.

The unidentified animal was in a pet carrier and looked like an extremely large raccoon with big, sharp teeth and an ugly hiss. He was wearing a harness and had been de-clawed, so I knew he was someone's "pet", but I did not know what kind of animal he was. All the neighbors rushed out of their houses to witness the excitement and offer their opinions.

After consulting the neighbors and researching the animal on the internet, we identified the animal as a Koatimundi from South America. They are apparently flesh-eating carnivores that scavenge for food in South America and are related to raccoons.

As we would find out later, this animal had a very storied history on its way to Perryton, Texas. He could have been very useful as a DEA agent if we could have deciphered his unsettling noises and hiss. He had been shifted from owner to owner as partial payment on "past due" drug accounts.

He weighed about forty pounds and was about three feet long from pointed nose to the tip of his ringed tail. Since we had never seen or been exposed to a Koatimundi before, we were both intimidated and curious. He was cute despite his big teeth and unnerving vocalization. He looked like a raccoon on steroids.

We determined he was the pet of a local drug dealer/entrepreneur. He had never been vaccinated for rabies and had to be placed in quarantine. John and I arrived at my office and developed a plan to transfer the overly excited animal from his small pet carrier to the larger quarantine cage.

The plan was for me to dump the animal in the cage at the same time John slammed the cage door closed. Although formulated in a hurry, this plan looked great on paper. Unfortunately, the plan worked much better on paper than it did in actuality.

As I poured the Koati out of the transport cage, John was his typically sluggish self and closed the kennel cage door slowly allowing the animal to escape into the clinic. He exited like a rocket.

I shouted at John to get his Animal Control Warden noose while I kept an eye on the animal, so it would not hide from us. As usual though, John had no equipment. I told him to watch the animal and not let him get out of his sight while I scurried into the kennel to get my noose.

When I returned, John was in a fetal position on top of the X-ray table and pointed down the hall yelling, "He went that way!"

So much for keeping his eyes on the speedy animal, which now had many rooms in which to hide. John's years of training and experience had served him well as he climbed up on the X-ray table to hide from the fleeing Koati.

John did get off the table to follow me down the hallway at a safe distance of about fifteen feet. After several minutes, I found the fractious animal in my office with papers and books thrown everywhere. I approached the animal with the 3-foot-long noose extended at arm's length, hoping for a quick snatch.

The animal then hissed, faked left, went right and made a sudden break for the door. Unfortunately, my athleticism was not an adequate match, and the Koati sped by me into the hallway, ending up face to face with John. John jumped into the bathroom, slamming and locking the door in one motion behind him.

He yelled through the bathroom door in an out of breath and shaky voice, "Have you got him yet, Doc? Doc? ... You got him? ... Hey, Doc, you out there?"

Despite the lack of help, I did finally secure the animal with superior skill, or more likely, with blind luck. John emerged from the bathroom covered in sweat and breathing hard only after I assured him that the animal was safely secured in the cage.

While I gave the Koati food and water, John stepped outside to smoke a cigarette and settle his nerves. He was still ghostly white when he returned several minutes later. As I started giving him a hard time about his lack of help and support, he chuckled and said he might not be cut out for this line of work. The same work that he had been trained for and done for the last several years.

During the quarantine, the Koati became quite a viewing attraction and settled in nicely. Many people dropped by the clinic to check him out. He was actually a very interesting animal that enjoyed human interaction and contact which made our capture experience even funnier.

By the end of the quarantine period, I was walking and petting the once "ferocious" animal. He was eating out of my hand rather than eating my hand. I think he was just terrified of the large, shaking, chain smoking Animal Control Officer who jumped from table to table, slammed and yelled through bathroom doors.

I'm sure the jumpy, domestic chore-smelling veterinarian didn't help settle his nerves any either. If you could control his occasional outburst and unpredictability, he would have been a great pet. (The Koatimundi that is .... not John).

The Koati went home without incident 10 days later to its original owner from out of town. Everyone in town was glad to be rid of the potential risk of future physical assaults from wild animals while emptying the trash. My wife was also glad because I have certainly used a lesser excuse in order to keep from emptying the trash.

That Koati excuse could have kept me off trash duty for years. Too bad for him, he didn't learn to hide in knee-high lawn grass because he could still be in my front yard, living undetected.

Loogied and Loaded

Exotic animals offer a break from the usual appointments of the day and are great fun to work on. They create new and exciting challenges and working on them is never uneventful. The first job I received after graduation from veterinary school was at Dr. Ron Easley's clinic in Pampa, Texas.

Ron had a healthy practice with a large group of owners with exotic animals. It was during an oil boom and many of the wealthy oil men had unique pets. Dr. Easley was the regional expert for exotic animals and many of the region's most challenging exotic animal cases were referred to him. As a result, I learned a lot working with him for a year.

Soon after starting and fresh after graduation, I got a call from a llama owner who had an emergency with one of his valuable females. The llama had lacerated her leg while trying to keep the stud away from her new baby. She kicked at the male and cut her leg on the sharp tin on the edge of the barn. She could not use the leg and it was bleeding profusely.

Though he lived several miles away, the owner had been referred to Dr. Easley in the past for his expertise. He wanted to skip the middleman and return to the best quickly because of the new mother's high value. I advised him to apply an antibiotic ointment under a pressure wrap and head to the clinic.

As I often did that first few months after graduation, I called Dr. Easley for advice. He volunteered to assist me in this case because of the rarity of the case and the llama's value. His willingness to assist was a great relief to me.

Ron seemed relieved as well. He was more relieved that I had called instead of diving in by myself on this expensive animal. While I have never been accused of possessing a lack of confidence, it was good to have a patient, experienced colleague to council me and allow me to tap into his large amount of knowledge. He was also a good friend, which made it even a better situation.

The llama arrived at the clinic just after dark and we went to work. Her right leg was lacerated just above and behind the ankle. The laceration was five inches long and deep. It had severed her Achilles tendon.

Since the tendon had been completely lacerated, she could not support weight on the leg. The pain and inability to use the leg made the llama frantic. She was uncooperative and antsy. We decided to fully anesthetize her in order to thoroughly flush and clean the wound before attempting to repair the tendon.

This was one of the rare occasions that I got to share something new with Dr. Easley. Before graduation, I was exposed to a new suturing technique used to repair ruptured tendons in horses. It was a great opportunity to use the technique to repair this tendon. Large tendons such as the Achilles are difficult to suture and get to heal properly. They are slow-healing and have a lot of force exerted on them during the healing process.

This surgery went very well because of the clean laceration and the quick response of the owner. Since not much time had elapsed since the injury, the tendon could be manipulated easily without excessive muscle contraction, making apposition more difficult. We used a large diameter, non-absorbable suture to repair the tendon. The laceration was clean, and the tendon, which was the size of a garden hose, came together nicely.

After surgically repairing the tendon and skin laceration, we placed a fiberglass cast on the leg. The cast stretched from above the knee to the hoof to keep the joints above and below the wound immobile. The cast would help the healing process by holding the leg perfectly still while the tendon mended.

The heavy, cumbersome cast also limited the llama's mobility because of its weight and size. She enjoyed planting the cast in the sand and pivoting on it for her own entertainment. I think she enjoyed making herself dizzy.

One of the enormous challenges faced in this case was the potential for infection.-Expense was not an issue with this valuable llama, and we could break out the good stuff. Unfortunately, the good stuff only came in an injection that had to be given daily in a large muscle mass.

This llama didn't have a large muscle mass. She was long and lean. The daily injections became my responsibility because Dr. Easley claimed it would be a wonderful learning experience. It certainly was a learning experience for me and good humor for Dr. Easley.

I arrived at the clinic fresh and excited in my khakis, dress shirt and tie the next morning for another exciting day at the office. I have long ago given up on wearing a tie to work. When I was young and fresh out of school, I felt the tie helped me appear more mature and improved my credibility with the pet owners. Now my old face and grey hair do the same.

As soon as I got to the clinic, I rushed to the barn to check on my new patient. She was standing up and looking good. The cast was not hot and there was no drainage or discharge to indicate infection. It appeared she had adapted well to her cast. She was nibbling on hay and looking after her new baby.

I walked to the fridge with a spring in my step and drew up her antibiotic injection. It was more of a celebratory dance than a walk. The antibiotic was moderately thick and difficult to draw into the syringe, but I was so happy, it didn't matter.

The thick antibiotic burns when it is injected and often provokes an angry response by the animal. The viscosity and slow injection time of the drug meant the pain response was prolonged. It is common to be bitten when giving this injection to dogs and cats. Horses try to kick, paw and snort at you. Llamas, as I found out, try to do something altogether different.

I crawled over the fence and gave my usual greeting to the llama. I rechecked the cast. Everything looked and felt great. I played with the baby llama a few minutes before giving the antibiotic injection to the mother. She did not seem to mind that I was messing with her newborn baby.

The baby llama soon grew tired of me, so I decided to get on with the day. I scoped out the usual injection sites for several minutes before deciding to give the shot in the hip of the injured leg. I rubbed the site for a few seconds to help numb the area where the needle would enter the skin. I pulled the cap off the needle with my teeth as usual and jabbed the needle deep into the llama's booty muscle.

She did not enjoy the burning sensation of the medication as it entered the muscle tissue. She spun round and round, pivoting on the leg with the cast. The foot remained in one spot, and she acted like a centrifuge around it.

While she spun, she started making a very unusual gargling sound. It was a sound that I had not heard before in my limited llama work. The sound was a deep growling noise that started in her abdomen and resonated through her throat.

As I soon discovered, she was hocking up a huge loogie! While I looked at the llama, trying to figure out what was going on, she fired a large, wet, nasty loogie right by my head. The wad shot by my ear and slammed with a thud against the metal barn wall.

I soon found out that llamas can spit loogies very quickly and effectively. She fired loogie after loogie in all directions while spinning on the planted leg. The llama mamma fired loogies like a machine gun. Some of the loogies landed direct hits on me while others pounded the barn wall, drug cabinets, closet doors, and windows.

Llama loogies hurt like heck when they hit you and they smell horrendous. The smell is nasty and long-lasting. It permeates your clothing, skin, office and car.

I scurried out of the pen and ducked for cover behind the chute. The large, sharp needle was slung in all directions as I dove to safety. I hunkered down like a World War I soldier in a bunker and waited for the barrage to end. I was covered in foul smelling nastiness from head to toe.

The damage was severe, and I needed a change of clothes. I for sure wasn't coming out until I heard no more loogies being launched. I waited several long minutes for the firing to stop. It is common for veterinarians to have large laundry bills because we are forced to change clothes early and often because of our messy jobs. However, this was probably a record time for me to already need a change of clothes.

Dr. Easley had also arrived early that morning and witnessed the entire event from the safety of the hallway window. He laughed so long and hard at me; it was embarrassing. Although he wouldn't admit it, I think he showed up early that day because he knew what would happen and wanted to catch all the carnage. I never knew him to show up early before or after that time. The carnage was a sight to see, and Ron really enjoyed it.

After the initial injection, I got much wiser. I put on coveralls, a coat, gloves and an ear-flapped hat before I gave the remaining injections. It took several days to get the smell of the loogies off my body and weeks to get the smell out of my coat.

The rest of the clinic staff also showed up early that entire week to view the treatment through the hallway window. Dr. Easley said it was a wonderful bonding experience for them and the best staff meetings ever. I was glad I could be of assistance.

The llama mamma and her baby both did very well. The tendon healed, and I removed the cast in a month. Other than a sore booty and a slight limp, the llama was back to normal.

Lion's Den

Late one Sunday afternoon, I received an emergency call from a man whose Collie was suffering with several large, nasty, open wounds. The seeping sores were infested with a huge number of nasty maggots. Even though it had been going on for several days and he noticed the maggots this morning, he waited to call until halftime of the late afternoon televised Dallas Cowboy's football game.

He was sure now that it was an emergency because he had a free 15 minutes during halftime. After agreeing it was an emergency, I offered to meet him at the clinic. He asked if we could wait until after the football game was over.

Several hours and an overtime game later, I met him and examined his dog. The wounds looked bad, as they were covered with maggots and had a nasty smell. I found the lesions to be superficial after a closer examination. They were allergic "hotspots" and confined to the back half of his body.

Allergic dermatitis or "hotspots" are common in animals whose allergies appear as skin rashes. These rashes commonly become infected and draw the attention of flies in the summer. The therapy involves shaving the hair off the infected lesions, giving a steroid injection, giving antibiotics and applying topical medications to the sores.

I explained that the therapy included shaving the infected area and that his Collie would resemble a lion with a mane when he picked him up the following day. He thought it would be "cool to have him look like a Detroit Lion."

***

The following Monday, I was blessed by a visit from one of my all-time favorite patients. Baxter was a full-grown African Lion that was owned by a local migratory cowgirl. She got the cub while traveling through Missouri and brought him home on a whim. Since she lived in the country, there were no city ordinances that prevented her from keeping the wild, exotic animal.

She tried to contain him inside a wooden fence near her rented house. He was a rambunctious kitten that destroyed whatever was in his path. No simple wooden fence could secure him. He continually got out and roamed the countryside hunting for adventure.

As a cub, Baxter had broadened my African Lion knowledge and the African Lion knowledge of several Texas A&M Veterinary School professors. On one of his excursions, Baxter did not return and was found several days later very ill with encephalitis. The brain infection was difficult to treat and probably made him less than a Rhodes Scholar when he recovered.

His care required a long and strenuous recovery with days of hospitalization and numerous consultations with the experts. His treatment was unusual, and he did not respond as we expected him to, but he did finally recover. Despite all the painful injections, catheters, IV fluids and venipunctures, Baxter and I somehow became good friends. When his owner would bring him to visit my office, he would destroy more and more of my waiting room with each visit.

He was a tremendous physical specimen that did what he pleased. After all, he was "King of the Texas Panhandle Jungle". We could not control him because of his enormous size and tremendous strength. On this day's visit, he shredded all the plants in my waiting room and put the clinic parrot through a stress test with a loud roar. Chuck left his perch and headed for the kennel.

On this Monday, Baxter came to the clinic to say goodbye and give it one last thrashing. He had certainly grown into "Lionhood" with a full mane and attitude. He sampled several bags of dog and cat food before mutilating all the plants and blinds. As the petite owner and I sat in the waiting room, trying to hold on to this large destructive force, I prayed that Mrs. Jones would be late for her appointment and didn't bolt through the front door with her 3-pound Chihuahua prancing in front of her. I'm sure the pint size pet would have become an after-dinner mint for Baxter.

As luck would have it, the next client that came through the front door wasn't Mrs. Jones, but was the dog's owner from the day before. He was shocked and surprised to be greeted by the slobbery lick of a full-grown African Lion across his face. As he wiped the slobber from his face and his eyes focused, he exclaimed in a shaky voice, "Boy, you weren't kidding when you said my dog would look like a lion when I picked him up!"

Unfortunately, as time went by, Baxter became too aggressive and too powerful to be trusted. His owner was forced to arrange for an alternative living arrangement. Baxter joined the ranks of a group of lions at a popular Las Vegas hotel. While it took him a while to adjust to the confinement and not being the only lion for miles around, he sure loved the lady lions. They helped tame the beast, and he adjusted well.

Persistent Pigeon

It is common in a small farming community for well-meaning people to bring in "injured" wildlife to be treated. Most of these animals are young animals that have been separated from their mothers and are not injured at all. Occasionally, these injuries are real and require veterinary care. I enjoy working with wildlife because it is unusual and fun. It also offers unique challenges.

The local game warden blesses me often with these treatment and rehabilitation challenges. The clinic staff and I enjoy the creativity of naming these animals with fitting names. We've had the scrawny baby owl found in a dog pen named Milkbone. A baby red-tailed hawk named Loogie for 'Hawk a Loogie' and an injured grebe named Flip for 'Flip the Bird'.

Most of these "injured" animals are infants that the mother has left temporarily. Human nature causes us to scoop these animals up and nurture them. Most of these infants are in good health and the mother is still taking care of them. It is always much better to leave wildlife where you find them.

After a thorough checkup, most of these animals can be returned to where they were found and resume their normal lives. The process of getting the animals back to and accepted by their mothers is the real challenge.

Perryton is located at the intersection of two major highways and gets many travelers coming through town. One hot August day at noon, a couple of travelers pulled into the clinic parking lot and intercepted me on my way to lunch. They had found an ill pigeon on the highway about seven miles south of town near a farmhouse and brought it all the way back to town for help.

This pigeon was definitely ill. He was showing the classic clinical signs of cyanide poisoning. Cyanide has not been available on the commercial market for several years because of its toxicity and potential human risk. It is a very effective poison and was used for years by farmers and ranchers to rid their farms of many different pests.

Old farmers still have ample supplies stored away to use on their toughest pests. Pigeons fit into this 'toughest pest category' based on their filth, noisiness, and persistence. Almost all farms have a large pigeon population which is very noxious and messy. These freeloading birds spread disease and create headaches for all farmers.

I promised the travelers I would do my best to help this pigeon with a "brain infection" get well. I gave them the infection diagnosis even though it was much lower on the differential diagnostic list. I didn't want the poor farmer being verbally abused for poisoning a pigeon by a couple of well-meaning, passionate tourists.

The tourists left with a spring in their step and a feeling of well-being for saving one of God's poor creatures from certain doom.

The pigeon responded well to the cyanide antidote and was back to normal in no time. He flew with determination and passion directly back to the farmhouse to continue tormenting the poor farmer.

The verbal abuse from the travelers might have been less painful for the poor farmer to take than the familiar, boastful coo he heard coming from the pigeon as he flew over the barn announcing his return. I'm sure the coffee shop stories of the pigeon with nine lives continue to grow with each telling. The seasoned farmers are left to wonder how their old, trusted cyanide could have let them down. Nine lives or not, that was one lucky pigeon, thanks to human nature.

Dr. Doolittle Has Nothing On Me

Clipping the flight feathers on pet birds is done regularly to prevent injury and escape. It is common for veterinarians to treat birds that haven't had their wings trimmed and have inadvertently flown into ceiling fans or smashed into windows.

Even the largest pet bird is no match for a Hunter Ceiling Fan running on high or a streak-free, double-paned storm window. I have treated everything from concussions to fractured appendages in these patients.

Handling birds can be very unpredictable and challenging. Since a large bird's beaks are made to crack tough nutshells, they pack a significant amount of force. A vet can suffer significant damage at the hands of one of these handling efforts.

Trimming flight feathers involves holding the bird reasonably still while trimming just enough of the large flight feathers on the wing. The goal is to prevent the birds from gaining altitude but still allow them to land softly. It's often a fine line between getting too much and not enough.

When not enough of the feather is trimmed, the bird can still fly. When too much of the feather is trimmed, the base can bleed profusely. Both occurrences can test a veterinarian's liability insurance. It is critical to warn the owner to not trust the trimming until the bird has been allowed to try and fly indoors. It is sickening to see your expensive bird fly off into the trees after a less than perfect wing trim.

This day's challenge at the office was to trim the flight feathers on a very large, beautiful, and ornery Macaw parrot named Gator.

Gator was a beautiful bird with a lot of personality which oozed out of him. He enjoyed talking. Talking birds mimic the phrases they hear the most, and Gator's favorite phrase was "Mom ... Mom ... Mom" in a child's voice that got progressively louder in a crescendo fashion.

An annoyed sounding "WHAT!" followed that phrase in an adult female voice.

There was no hiding of family secrets with Gator. He apparently heard this exchange around the house quite often.

Gator's trips to the vet office are usually quick because of the loud, constant "Mom ... Mom ... Mom ... WHAT!" that resonates through the office.

We got him in and out in a hurry because it's annoying.

Most people feel they see human characteristics in their pets. It's often easy to tell what a pet is thinking in my office. It was easy to tell what Gator was feeling because he told you most of the time.

When we catch Gator and begin his wing trim, he takes on a human characteristic. He shrieks in a loud cry, "HELP ME ... HELP ME ... MOM ... HELP ME ... HELP ME ... MOM". It is humorous and unsettling all at the same time.

The best thing is seeing the look on the client's face in the next room when I enter after trimming Gator's feathers. They can't help but hear the entire exchange through the walls. First-time clients wonder if I'm also a pediatrician and long-term clients wonder if I'm expanding my practice to include treating wild children.

It's fortunate that Gator is the only patient with whom I can have a two-way vocal conversation. I'm glad my other patients can't talk even though it would make diagnosing easier. I suspect most of them wouldn't stop at telling me where it hurts. They would also tell me where to stick it.

Sound-mimicking birds can also present some unusual difficulties for my profession. Every few years, I read a story about a bird with a chronic cough in the veterinary journals. After loads of tests and hundreds of dollars, the veterinarian discovers the bird lives in the same house as a smoker.

He is just mimicking the sound he constantly hears. As a result, the first question I asked about coughing birds is, "Does anyone in the house smoke?"

Part Two: Dogs and Cats

Slow Learner or Anesthetic Addict?

Porcupines are cute animals with a unique defense mechanism. They are covered with a modified type of hair called quills. These quills are rigid, sharp and microscopically barbed. The sharp quills resemble toothpicks and stand up when the porcupines are afraid or harassed by a predator. Porcupines use these quills effectively to defend themselves.

When a predator attacks and bites the porcupine, the sharp quills jab into and remain in the tissues they contact. It is very painful for the predator because the quills penetrate deep into the tissues and are covered with reactive skin oils and dirt. These additives make the penetrated area itch intensely.

The quills lodge in the predator's mouth as they try to bite the porcupines. Porcupines are also very effective at slapping with their tails and leaving quills behind. The quills cause a great deal of pain and prevent the animal from eating, drinking or swallowing if there are many of them. Quilled dogs drool and scratch vigorously at their mouth and face which often causes the quills to enter their legs and feet.

The most common domestic animals that get exposed to porcupines are dogs, but I have removed quills from cattle, horses, cats and pigs. Dogs usually have quills in their face, mouths and front legs. The other animals usually get quills in their noses and front legs as they examine the strange-looking porcupines.

Tejas lived on Wolf Creek near Lake Fryer which gave him ample opportunities to take part in has favorite pastime of chasing wild animals. The area is rich in wildlife and Tejas loved to chase and harass them all. He was a very active Border Collie-mix, full of energy. He treasured the secluded life which provided access to all sorts of playmates. Not all his newfound playmates cared as much about playing with him. Many porcupines inhabited the wooded areas around the creek.

I'm certain that Tejas holds the record for the number of times that quills had to be removed. At least he holds the record for quill removal events in the Western Hemisphere. At last count, he was up to 48 times. So many times, in fact, that he could possibly be classified as a slow learner. On the other hand, I think he really enjoyed the anesthetic I used to remove the quills.

Most of the time, quill removal requires placing the animal under general anesthesia and plucking the quills out one by one. This process is too painful to be done with the animal awake. The quills are grasped with forceps and tugged out in the same direction that they enter.

Some quills work their way under the skin or break off below the skin's surface and are almost impossible to remove. These quills migrate around under the skin for a few days before working their way out. Because of the barbs, the quills can only travel in one direction.

The quills are very sharp and reactive, which makes the animals miserable. They need a strong round of antibiotics to prevent infection. Pain medicines are also needed to control the animal's discomfort.

Every time I remove quills, I stick myself several times. This means that I could be classified as a slow learner as well. The puncture wounds burn and itch and cause large, red bumps on my skin. They hurt like the dickens.

Removed quills are a big hit at school programs. I enjoy showing them off because the school kids think the quills are just "too cool, man". I always have the kids try to guess what they think the quills could be. Guesses have been all sorts of things. Many of the kids guess toothpicks or bird bones.

One rather loud child guessed it was a snake's wiener at one school program. I'm pretty sure that guess was made so he could say the word "wiener". From the moans and groans of his classmates, I could tell it wasn't the first time he had spoken of wieners.

Tejas' desire to continue confronting porcupines perplexed me. His owner and I have discussed several times what compelled him to continue his porcupine pursuits. Her guess is as good as mine. She likes to think it is his overwhelming sense of defending his territory. I still think it has to be one of two reasons; he loved balding porcupines, or he was addicted to the anesthetic.

Weiner Biter Weimaraner

Like most of the Weimaraner dogs that come into the clinic, Dakota was a bundle of energy and excitement. Her energy and excitement level were so high that other Weimaraner's told her to calm down. Her excitement level was higher than even the most hyperactive Weimaraner on caffeine.

She couldn't stand still and was frantic in checking out everything and everyone. Her exuberance made having a normal conversation with her mild-mannered owner out of the question. His deep, low voice was barely audible over the racket she made while slamming around the exam room. She resembled a racket ball bouncing off the walls.

Dakota must have been easily excitable at home as well. She was injury-prone. I saw her for several traumatic injuries during her adolescences. She suffered through many sprains and bruises from being so active and curious. She was into everything.

Being so curious created problems for her. When she placed her front feet on the stovetop to check on dinner, she had a rude awakening. Her front feet landed squarely on the scorching hot burners. Both of her front paws received blistering burns. The painful burns did not slow her down any. She thought the foot wraps were cool and enjoyed showing them off. She waved them for everyone to see.

Not long after she tried to fry her feet, she came to the office with a deep laceration on the bottom of her chest. The deep wound looked as if she had stabbed herself in the chest with a long, sharp object. The jagged object punctured the skin and lacerated deep into the muscles of her ventral chest.

Despite bleeding profusely and muscle tissue hanging out of her chest wound, Dakota was as happy and active as ever. As she bounced off the walls in the exam room, blood splattered everywhere. There were even blood droplets on the ceiling tiles.

Dakota needed general anesthesia this time. I sent Mr. Davis home to find and remove the sharp object from the yard because I knew she would find it again. Dakota was a much better dog under anesthesia. She was calm and cuddly.

The large wound took a long time to clean and repair. It was packed with grass and dirt. I scrubbed, flushed, and sutured muscle and subcutaneous layers with absorbable suture, then trimmed and sutured the skin with a strong non-absorbable suture. The entire chest area was swollen and bruised because of the impact. She had used a lot of force trying to impale herself.

Despite the large wound and bruising, the chest healed well. Unfortunately, Mr. Davis could not find the sharp object that caused the wound, despite covering the yard from every angle. Dakota was the only one that knew the source of the trauma and she was too preoccupied with life to tell us.

Since there was no obvious source that we could find for the wound, we worried about potential foul play. It certainly would not be unheard of to have a dog with Dakota's energy level and loud bark be targeted by the neighbors. Undoubtedly, she probably made a lot of noise night and day. Despite further investigation, the cause of the injury remained a mystery.

Not long after the first wound healed, Dakota returned to the office for an emergency call with almost the same wound. The wound was in the same area and was approximately the same depth. Like before, it bled profusely and had tissue hanging out of the wound. Since the wounds were so similar, it helped to lessen our fears that the wounds were of human origin.

The wounds had to be caused by the same accident that had occurred a few weeks earlier. We repeated the wound treatment process with the same results. The wound healed quickly and well. All she had to show for the experience was a big scar.

Because of her injuries, Dakota came to the office often. She became very comfortable with her surroundings at the office. With each trip to the office to check her progress, Dakota would develop a new trick to show off.

She would chase her stubby tail, tug on her leash or throw head back and howl. None of these were as funny or impressive to us as the last nasty vice she developed and maintained. Mr. Davis was not as impressed with her new trick as we were. The first time she broke out this new trick, it was a total shock to the calm owner.

Weimaraner's are big dogs with big teeth. With their excitement and tendency to chew on everything as puppies, they can get your attention in a hurry. Dakota's newest vice was stealthy, and it grabbed your total, undivided attention immediately.

Poor Mr. Davis never saw the new trick coming. As he tried to explain her latest exploits in his quiet voice with his arms crossed on his chest, Dakota attacked him in mid-sentence. She reached up and clamped down hard on his crotch without warning. His voice suddenly went from a low mellow tone to a high-pitched shriek.

"I can't get her to ... CALM DOWN AT ALL," he chirped as his eyes got bigger than saucers.

His voice raised several octaves and went a high register. The volume increased several decibels as the dog's teeth clamped down. He tried to push her head away, but she held on. She then played tug-o-war with his business. She rocked her head back and forth like his unit was a dirty sock.

Her attempt was successful. She had got his undivided attention. Mr. Davis wiggled and danced as he tried to free his wiener from the dog's death grip. I tried not to laugh out loud, but it was funny, and I couldn't help myself. He finally broke the dog's death grip on his family jewels and continued on with his conversation while I laughed.

"She is so friendly but ... SO INCREDIBLY ACTIVE AND INTO EVERYTHING!" His voice raised several octaves again as Dakota came out of nowhere to grab his Johnson again.

Dakota was very slick and unpredictable with her new vice. She gave no warning before clamping down on his twig and berries. She did this several more times during the visit and I laughed each time because it was so funny. I think she thought it was funny as well. She would watch and wait until it was a great time to change his volume and tone.

I laughed way too long and too hard but couldn't help myself. It was hilarious. Through my laughter, I tried to help, advising him that either he had to invest in obedience training for Dakota or invest in a protective cup for himself.

A Tumor That Owns a Pet

I have been blessed since childhood with an overabundance of self-confidence. Even though I know I can handle whatever comes my way, there are a few clients who intimidate me.

One of the scariest was an elderly, 100-pound, ornery grandmother. She was meaner than a junkyard dog and could out-curse any sailor she met. Despite her small stature, she could make the manliest of men wet his pants.

Martha had retired from her stressful job as the head surgical nurse in a busy metropolitan hospital and moved to Perryton to be near her son, who was the local county judge. Martha was never afraid to shout out what she was thinking, no matter who it offended.

Like most people, she had a pet that matched her personality. She had an old, cranky Dachshund, Prissy, that barked, howled and growled at things that bothered her. During exams at my office, I did things that bothered her. With every vaccination or nail trim, Martha and Prissy would both call me names and insult my lineage.

It had been quite some time since I had seen Prissy when she showed up at my office with a big problem. Prissy arrived at her appointment with a unique appearance. Her normally long and skinny body bulged to the max at its midpoint. She looked distressed and very uncomfortable.

Martha knew there was something seriously wrong with her, but didn't want to face that fact and bring her in sooner. The mass in her abdomen was so large that it was not allowing Prissy to eat normally. The lack of caloric intake caused her to become weak and thin.

I tried to break the bad news that Martha already knew was coming. Prissy had a very large abdominal tumor that was growing rapidly. The cancer's growth appeared to be very aggressive.

The news was doubly depressing for Martha because the surgery would be expensive, and she did not have the cash to pursue therapy. As Martha and I discussed surgical therapy and the potentially poor prognosis for recovery, the Judge arrived to lend emotional and financial support to his elderly mother. He volunteered to pay for the entire surgery and follow-up care.

The surgery would not be easy on Prissy. She was weak, and the tumor was huge. I explained that the surgery was risky, but it was our only chance at treatment success. Martha agreed we should try, even though success was estimated at less than 25%.

Since the longer we waited before surgery, the weaker Prissy would get, we did the surgery that day. Martha left Prissy in my arms and said, "Don't kill my dog in surgery, you mean old bastard!"

I knew what she really meant to say was, "Good luck with Prissy's surgery! I know you will do your best and I'm confident in your abilities."

The preparation for surgery was a quick one as we placed an IV and scrubbed the stomach. We needed to move quickly to decrease the time Prissy would be under anesthesia. Abdominal tumors are seldom easy to remove, regardless of their size, but this one was going to be tough because of its girth.

Tumor removal surgeries are slow and tedious because of the growth's unpredictable blood supply and location next to vital organs. The need to prevent blood loss by suturing all the vessels that go to the abnormal tissue makes for slow work. Extra time is needed to remove all the diseased tissue. With Prissy's age and condition, I planned to take all the time I needed to remove the tumor, but not a second more.

I approached this tumor through a ventral abdominal incision. The tumor appeared to originate from the vascular base of the small intestines. Abdominal omentum had adhered to the mass and needed to be dissected free. The blood supply to the mass was profuse, and the vessels were huge.

The tumor was growing at a remarkably rapid rate. Through a slow, steady process, I teased it free from the vital abdominal structures and ligated the blood vessels supplying the mass one by one.

Once removed, the cancerous mass weighed 3 pounds. Prissy only weighed 10 pounds before surgery. It was an extreme tummy-tuck, and Prissy looked very stealthy after the surgery. Her recovery from the anesthetic was prolonged but uneventful.

She experienced a lot of pain because of the long abdominal incision which stretched from her sternum to the base of her pelvis. We tried to control her pain and build her strength over the next few days. Slowly, she improved. Martha visited daily to help lift Prissy's spirits and encourage her to get well.

She departed with comments such as, "Don't let that mean old doctor give you any crap. Just bite him."

The surgery was a total success. Without the tumor filling her abdomen, Prissy began to eat and regained her strength. While her recovery was slow, it was complete, and she was soon ready to go home.

During the discharge visit, I explained the home care instructions to Martha while she appeared to ignore me. She spent the time loving on and conversing with her happy pet. I continued to go over the instructions, even though I knew it was to no avail. She would just have to read the instructions when she got home and call if she had questions.

As Martha left, she surprised me so much that I thought I would faint. She turned to me, grabbed me in a bear hug and stated, "Thank you for saving Prissy's life! You are a great vet."

My lower jaw dropped to the floor. The warm fuzzy feeling did not last long as she turned to Prissy and said, "Let's get out of here before that son of a bitch tries to give you another shot."

RANDY L. SKAGGS, DVM

Bat Dog

Dogs are like superheroes. They possess senses that are superior to their human counterparts. They are blessed with amazing hearing and olfactory abilities. Their auditory systems capture a much broader range of sound waves than the human system.

Their ears can pick up the slightest sounds from great distances away. Dogs' ears can detect much higher and lower frequencies than human ears. They easily pick up the subtle, unique sounds of their owner's approaching car from blocks away or the sounds of storms approaching way off in the distance.

A dog's sense of smell is anywhere from 10,000 to 15,000,000 times better than ours, depending on their breed. This magnificently developed sense of smell allows them to do amazing things like detect cancer, track lost kids, and sniff out drugs. Specific training with positive reinforcement can cause dogs to further develop their skills in detecting certain odors.

It is said that when we come home, we can smell stew cooking on the stove. When dogs come home, they can detect the potatoes, carrots, onions, corn and each seasoning used in the stew.

I'm sure this superior olfactory system also causes them great pain at times. When your buddy passes gas in the car and the smell is causing you to gag, just think of poor old Fido in the back seat and feel his pain.

The general rule of thumb is the longer the dog's nose, the better his sense of smell. On the other hand, ear size doesn't seem to matter in a dog's ability to hear well. Attitude, intelligence and personality play a big role in whether a dog wants to be good with their God-given talents.

Some dogs are too lazy to put out that much effort. Other dogs are too dull to know the difference between a French fry and French poodle. Still others are too self-centered to get involved unless it benefits them.

KiKi seemed to be each of those dogs. She was one of those Boston Terrier dogs that looked much older than she was. She looked geriatric to me the first time I saw her, although she was only middle-aged. KiKi had the geriatric personality to match. Rarely did I ever see her show any kind of excitement or happiness. Instead, she wore a constant look of disdain and disapproval. This appearance worsened as she became geriatric.

Despite her lack of endearment for other people, she loved her owner. Jimmy got KiKi soon after becoming a bachelor and they planned to grow old together in his large, older home. His house was beautiful on the outside and was in a portion of town where many wealthy homeowners lived. The homes were older, but huge.

They were very well constructed, stood the test of time, and were surrounded by large trees. The houses were 60-90 years old and in neighborhoods which surrounded the old high school. This subdivision was where the wealthiest community members lived for many years.

KiKi lost her vision and hearing as she aged. As long as Jimmy didn't rearrange the furniture or do any big remodeling, she did great. She remained functional, but it took more effort to wake her up from naps or get her attention from a distance. I think some of this was selective hearing because she responded well to Jimmy's quiet voice at the office.

Jimmy's complaint was an unusual one on this day. "Doc, KiKi is doing the weirdest thing. She spends most of the day and night sleeping, but along about the same time each night she freaks out. She howls, barks and runs around the house whining."

Kiki's history, physical and ear exam turned up nothing. The behavior was strange with an unusual description. Since this behavior happened at the same time each night, I figured there must be something in her environment that stirred her up. It didn't fit the usual picture of seizure activity. There sure didn't appear to be any medical problem causing the behavior. It stumped me.

We couldn't stop there because this problem was driving both Jimmy and KiKi crazy. I prescribed KiKi a small dose of Valium for the evening and I gave Jimmy some homework. He was to go home and document the exact time of the event, what he heard or saw, and locate where KiKi's attention was focused at the time of the behavior.

Several days passed before I saw Jimmy again. He had gathered little new information. KiKi continued her nightly episodes of excitement, which seemed to occur at sundown and last for 15 minutes. She ran wildly through the house without focusing on one thing or area. The Valium seemed to help when he remembered to give it. The source of her anxiety remained a mystery at this point. It wasn't until a few weeks later that we found the cause.

Jimmy was having duct issues with his air conditioner in the attic. He called the technicians from William's Heating and Air Conditioning to fix it. Once they popped open the attic access of his house, the answer to KiKi's behavior was obvious. The large attic was packed wall to wall with bats. There were both live bats and dead bats everywhere. Huge piles of bat guano piled up over the ceiling joist.

It was easy to determine the origin of the bats. When the renovation of the old high school began, the bats were dislodged from their usual habitat. The old building was built in 1918 and housed all sorts of creatures, from bats to pigeons to huge rats.

When demolition began, these creatures were displaced and had to find new homes. The pigeons and the rats set up a new beginning in the old Perryton Equity grain silos across the road from the school. Apparently, the bats preferred the better, more refined real estate of Jimmy's attic.

The bats entered the house through a couple of damaged vents on each end of the attic. Like most unwanted house guests, they were messy. Jimmy's sense of smell must have been less than other humans. It's amazing that he didn't smell the huge mounds of bat guano. Undoubtedly, KiKi's powerful sense of smell picked it up and probably contributed to her grumpy outlook on life.

Each night at sundown, the nocturnal bats became active and made a mass exodus from the attic. Their rustling and high-pitched sounds could be heard by Kiki's sensitive ears, and it drove her crazy. The bats' exit only took a few minutes, after which KiKi could settle back down. The noises of the thousands of bats which were unperceived by human ears sounded like a huge invasion in her ears.

The bats grossed Jimmy out and drove him crazy once he knew they were there. He spent the next few days trying to evict the hordes of bats. They were persistent in wanting to stay, but he kept up the effort. He used constant bright lights, loud music, and continuous harassment. The bats eventually moved out.

The troublesome part came in trying to remove the piles of guano. The attic had to be gutted, disinfected and re-insulated. As a result, there is not a single crevice, crack or crease available for a bat's entry into Jimmy and KiKi's attic now. Kiki sleeps like a log now with no need for Valium.

Sounds Like a Personal Problem

Emergency calls in the middle of the night keep me wide awake and make it difficult for me to go back to sleep. I often wonder when other people sleep because a sizeable amount of us apparently watch our pets all night long.

The other calls that annoy me are the ones that occur right after I get home from a long day's work and I'm getting caught up on what happened during my girls' school day. Most of the time, these emergencies have been going on all day or for several days, but become very important after closing.

I had just arrived home from a very long day at the office when the phone rang as soon as I entered the door. The older lady on the line was very apologetic for calling after hours, but was also frantic. All day long, her Schnauzer had been having "serious problems". She couldn't put her finger on the diagnosis, but the clinical signs sounded serious to her.

"Megan is running around the house, hiding, howling, rubbing her rear on the carpet and biting under her tail. She is acting just like I would if my bowels were impacted!" she exclaimed with an excited shrill. "I just know you need to see her right now!"

In the animal world, there are clinical signs that are classical and very common and make the diagnosis easy. Megan's activities are classical clinical signs of impacted anal glands. Anal glands produce a pungent-smelling fluid that helps dogs mark their territory and lubricate the tissues when they pass a stool. They are the same glands that skunks use to defend themselves so effectively.

Fortunately, dog glands do not smell as bad, nor do they have a spraying capability. When they become full and infected, the poor dogs are miserable and really need help. I agreed to meet her at the clinic to give Megan some relief.

I had a tough time keeping a straight face while examining the dog and correcting her infected anal glands. I had visions of what Karen would act like if her bowels were impacted. The older, plus-sized woman would be running frantically downtown, howling, hiding, licking her rear and rubbing her butt on the carpet at the local lady's dress boutique. All because she needed a large dose of Exlax.

I called the local physician, Dr. Siewert, the next day to fill him in on what to watch for in case of a suspected case of impacted bowels in Karen. I figured I could enlighten him and save him some time in diagnosing and treating Karen if he saw these symptoms. But on the other hand, he may already know these signs because they may be classical and common clinical signs in humans with impacted bowels.

Part Three:
Livestock

Jerry's Rule

Jerry's Rule is named after one of my all-time favorite clients. Jerry Blasingame was a retired teacher who owned a herd of cattle with his son. His son was a successful local banker. It is amazing that many successful community leaders are the children of teachers. Teachers are by far the most successful profession at raising successful children.

Jerry was the type of guy that could brighten even the worst day with his humor and contagious laughter. He could take the kidding as well as he could dish it out. He was as good as they get, and I have missed interacting with him since his death because of cancer several years ago.

Jerry's cattle were large and barely fit into the extra-large chute at my office. Jerry was once a good cowboy but, as he got older and his son got busier, he would bring the cows into the office at the first sign of calving trouble. He claimed he didn't want to get in over his head with no help nearby. I think he came in just to harass me frequently.

Since his cows were so large, they seldom needed much help except straightening out a folded leg or a turned head and pulling the calf. It was usually quick work, and the biggest challenge was carrying the 125-pound calf to the trailer. The deliveries of these large calves occurred back when I was much younger and had much more energy, so they didn't bother me much.

While most of these births were unremarkable and didn't create a specific memory, there was one that I remember well. I could tell by the bulky leg protruding from the cow's back end that the calf was large. It appeared larger than it actually was because of the swelling that occurs when the calf's legs or face are wedged in the birth canal for an extended period.

The swelling occurs because the calf's heart continues to pump arterial blood into the tissue while the pressure constricts the weaker veins. The longer the calf spends in the cow's pelvic canal, the more swelling occurs. Some calves have difficulty nursing the first day because of this swelling.

This cow was older and had a very spacious pelvis. We coaxed her into the squeeze chute and gave her an epidural to ease the pain and stop the straining. I was busy with small animal appointments in the front of the clinic and rushed to deliver the emergency.

At this point in my career, I was very self-confident and was always in a hurry. I often rushed just to rush. I thought by rushing that it would create some free time in the day.

Actually, the opposite occurred. The faster I completed a task, meant that there would be more time to do more work. None the less, I whipped through my day with vigor, chasing a moment of solitude and a sense of accomplishment. This day was no exception.

I gloved up and evaluated the problem. The most common presentation of a calf in delivery is with both front legs and head in the birth canal. They look like they is diving into a swimming pool. The problem in this calf's delivery was a common one. He had a front leg folded back into the uterus. The technical name is dystocia.

This causes an impossible natural delivery for the cow unless the leg straightens out. The calf can only pass so far through the birth canal without the other leg being in the correct position. He bottlenecks at the interior pelvic opening, which creates pain and problems for the cow.

This birthing problem is easily corrected by pushing the calf's head and leg back into the uterus and straightening out the bent leg. The epidural helps stop the cow from pushing back on the calf and being counterproductive as the calf's presentation is corrected.

Once the calf is in the correct presentation, the birthing chains are placed on the legs and the calf can be gently pulled through the birth canal. Since this cow's birth canal was large enough to drive a Honda through, the calf came out quickly with little effort on my part.

The calf was weak because of the delay in his arrival but responded quickly to oxygen and pepped right up. He weighed 127 pounds according to his hoof measurement. Since he was so large, I didn't even consider the possibility that he might be a twin.

As a result, I didn't spend the time to glove back up and check. Twins are usually a scrawny 50 to 60 pounds and delivered without requiring help. Occasionally, the twins will battle over who gets to come out first and create a dystocia.

After a few minutes of oxygen, Jerry's calf was doing great and ready to go. We lugged the huge calf to the trailer and loaded the cow behind him. Jerry was happy and took off to return his fresh addition to the herd. I was just as happy because I didn't get too slimy and could go back to work on my small animal appointments with minimal cleaning.

It was several days later before I discovered the need to implement "Jerry's Rule". Jerry spent most afternoons at a local convenient store drinking coffee and chewing the fat with his retired buddies. I would stop in occasionally to enjoy the company.

A few days after pulling the calf for Jerry, I stopped by the "Gas-N-Stuff" to get an overly large diet coke and take some harassment from Jerry's gang. They enjoyed picking on me and I enjoyed their humor. It was generally very predictable, but sometimes they flashed their creative genius and made me belly laugh.

As I walked in, Jerry met me with his usual greeting, "Hey, how's it going, Dr. Death?"

His voice was loud and resonated through the busy store as people turned to join in the fun. I had earned this name from Jerry when we tried to nurture a group of old, malnourished, bank-repossessed cows back to health and through the calving season. Even though most of them made it, Jerry liked to remind me of the ones that didn't.

I knew something was up by the chuckles and excited looks on the faces of Jerry's buddies when I walked in. You could tell that they had been planning this for some time. Jerry was patient and slow with his delivery, like he had practiced it several times.

"Hey Dr. D, I'm only gonna pay you half of yer vet bill for delivering that calf the other day!" he stated in his loud, slow drawl.

I waited some time for the punch line. I had time to ice and fill my 44-ounce Diet Dr. Pepper before he continued.

"When I got to the farm, that cow had another calf in the trailer!" The table burst into laughter as they waited for my reaction.

I had to laugh at their reaction. I assured him that if I had known about that, I would have charged him twice as much. It was humorous because all ended well. Both calves were alive and doing well. The second calf was about half the size of the first. He probably hit the side of the trailer at Mach 5 when he shot out of the wide birth canal like a rocket.

Because of this slipup on my part, Jerry's Rule came to life. Jerry's Rule states that no cow leaves the chute after a deliver that is not checked for another calf. The rule applies if the calf weighs 50 or 150 pounds. The rule has paid off more than once and is one to live by. We should post it in every vet clinic in the United States.

Don't Eat the Pork

Pigs are challenging animals to examine and treat. They are stout animals with low centers of gravity and don't enjoy being handled. It would be great if God had designed them with handles.

Baby pigs rapidly pass the size where you can grab an ear with one hand and poke a shot in them with the other. The next step up requires more skill but can be used on any size hog. It involves catching the pig's nose in a snout rope to hold them still.

Attaching a snout rope is a skill that takes a lot of time to master. It involves looping a rope or cable snare around the pig's nose and upper jaw and quickly pulling it tight. The rope tightens around the nose and upper jaw behind the pig's large front teeth. The trick is to get the rope positioned where the pig will open its mouth, so you don't also encircle the lower jaw.

If the rope goes around the lower jaw, the rope slips off the funnel-shaped face. It also means that the operator will probably fall on his rump as he pulls to hold the retreating pig. As the rope slips off, the landing is hard and smelly because you always land in piles of fresh hog poop.

Once the snout is caught and the rope is tightened, the screaming begins. The sound is high-pitched, loud and painful to the ears. It's like being next to the speakers in the mosh pit at a Led Zeppelin concert. The squeals are piercing and make your eardrums feel like they are rupturing.

A normal response would be to drop everything in your hands and cover your ears. Most sane people scurry off with their fingers, plugging their ear holes. All that's left behind are partially deaf veterinarians and spouses that are used to their significant others yelling at them.

Show pigs are the most challenging group to treat because they have seen it all in their brief lives. They know that nothing good happens when the snout rope is applied. The crafty pigs know exactly what a snout rope is and how to avoid getting caught with it.

They dip, duck and juke from one side of the pen to the other. These crafty moves leave the snout roper catching nothing but air. All the while, the other pigs in the pen are chewing on your shoes and pant legs or darting between your legs. The pen mates pound your shins and knees.

Once the pig is caught, it's critical to move quickly, hoping to save what's left of your hearing.

Shots can be given quickly and smoothly. Drawing blood samples requires more time and sometimes protective ear plugs. In order to get a large blood sample for testing, you have to draw from one of the large veins deep in the pig's neck. A large-gauge, six-inch needle is used to poke and hunt until the vein is located.

"Poking and hunting" describes the technique. It's kind of like drilling for oil. All the while, your head is next to the pig's voice box that's destroying your auditory complexes with its high-pitched squeal.

Students that graduate from vet school have no experience catching pigs or hitting their blood vessels. Since I grew up raising show pigs, I probably had more experience than anyone, but I wasn't going to volunteer to demonstrate.

The graduate veterinary student that drew the short straw taught the lesson on drawing blood. He started by slowly reading the literature on how to bleed a pig. I couldn't tell if it was his first time to read it or if he was wasting as much time as possible before starting. He went over the documented approach to the vein while all 128 students sat in the bleachers and watched from a long distance away.

After a struggle to catch the pig in a snout rope, the grad student poked and jabbed and poked and jabbed and finally gave up after a few minutes. The students didn't care because 90% of the class never expected to treat a pig and 100% of us were glad the squealing had stopped. The poor grad student shouldn't have felt bad because it's not a simple task. It becomes easier when you've done it a thousand times.

The approach is based less on the anatomical guidelines and more on the "feel" of the needle as it hits certain structures in the neck. Trial and error teach you how these structures feel and which way to move the needle to find the correct location. That being said, sometimes a pig will not give you a single drop of blood, no matter how hard you poke.

Most show pigs must be bled at least once for certain infectious diseases and each new year brings fresh adventures in treating them. Besides pneumonia and diarrhea, seldom does each year have the same diseases to treat.

I remember one particular year as a strange one. Many show pigs were battling brain and spinal cord infections because of a Staphylococcus bacteria. The infection spread rapidly through the 4-H and FFA barns. Surprisingly, most of the pigs responded well to therapy with the appropriate medications.

Unfortunately, a couple of pigs were treated for several days with the wrong medications by the Ag teacher and the local "pig expert" before I got to check them. It always surprises me that someone will spend $1,200.00 on a show pig and not seek professional help when they become ill.

One of these poor pigs was way beyond saving. He had been down for 10 days and could not stand or eat. His equilibrium was off because of the infection, and his world was spinning out of control. He rolled from one side of his pen to the other while his eyes spun in their sockets.

Seeping sores were present on his shoulders and hips from being down for so long. He was miserable, and we treated him with the entire medicine cabinet, to no avail. The damage to his fragile nervous system was severe and beyond repair.

After a few days of trying everything to save him, we were forced to admit defeat. He needed to be put out of his misery. The owners wanted to euthanize the pig by injection instead of using a firearm. Even though a well-trained person with a firearm can euthanize an animal quickly and painlessly with a single shot, many people can't bring themselves to use this method.

Euthanasia solutions injected in a vein work well in most species. These solutions are concentrated doses of the same medications used for surgical anesthesia. The high concentration of barbiturates essentially causes an overdose, which shuts down the heart and breathing centers. The animals usually pass away in a few seconds.

On the contrary, pigs don't respond well to anesthetics, or the drugs used to euthanize them. They have a high tolerance for most of the available medications. As a result, these drugs just don't work well in hogs. Despite being deathly ill, this pig was no different.

I took extra vials of the euthanasia solution because I knew it was going to be difficult. The pig weighed about 125 pounds and should have required about 15 milliliters of the thick pink medicine to put it down. Experience told me that dose wouldn't even scratch the surface. I gave 30 milliliters with the first dose. After a few minutes filled with continual grunts from the pig, I gave 30 milliliters more with the second dose.

A few more minutes passed with less vigorous grunts from the pig, and I gave 40 milliliters with a third dose. The pig appeared to be sleeping soundly with loud snoring, but was still alive. Finally, the pig gave up after the last 50 milliliter dose and breathed his last. The final tally was 10-times the label dose needed to put him down.

After the plethora of shots and tears by the owners, we were faced with how to dispose of the animal. The sizeable crowd that had gathered to watch the carnage discussed several options. Several recommended dumping the carcass in a city dumpster in a secluded area. Thankfully, the ladies who probably have to carry out the trash at their houses nixed that idea.

I offered my legally responsible idea of the traveling "dead truck". The "dead truck" will come by and pick carcasses up for a fee. This fee is hefty for anything but cattle because they use the cattle carcasses to make "Beef and More" dog food. The company explains that they can only have so much "More" in each bag of dog food to satisfy the government. As a result, pigs require a $75 charge for removal. This was too steep for the pig's owners.

Someone in the crowd had a friend that lived in the country who agreed to let them to throw the pig into a canyon on his land. He planned to use the pig carcass to attract coyotes, which he could shoot from a distance. Ranchers often use dead animals to attract the aggressive coyotes for elimination.

The coyotes cause large amounts of financial loss and distress to the ranchers when they attack and eat baby calves. It sounded like a win-win situation. It turned out to be much more than that.

By the time the owners drank a few more beers and got the pig deposited in the canyon, it was very late. The landowner stumbled out the next morning to find the partially eaten dead pig with three dead coyotes on the ground beside it. A fourth coyote rested next to the others stoned out of his gourd. They had eaten their fill of the pig carcass and received a lethal, secondhand dose of barbiturates that laid them out cold.

Hearing this story made me realize I'd missed an opportunity. I could have charged him four times as much if I'd known the carnage I was going to create. In retrospect, I'm glad they chose the option of coyote bait instead of "Beef and More' dog food. The "More" part in that bag might have killed a dog or two.

That's No "Mad Cow", But She Sure Is Ticked Off

The emergency call rang late on a cool night in the spring. The caller was an extremely nice young rancher who was having some difficulties with a cow delivering her calf. I agreed to meet him at the office after his 30-minute drive to town.

His lengthy trip gave me the time needed to open the barn and get things set up to deliver the calf. It also allowed me to be sure all the gates and doors were securely closed because Eric's cattle were usually rambunctious. They tested the welds on all the fences.

Eric pulled into the clinic, displaying the sheepish grin that was always on his face. He's a slow moving, even-tempered cowboy who never speaks above a whisper.

"Doc, you might want to watch her because she's a bit on the waspy side. She is definitely on the prod."

The translation of this cowboy lingo is "she will tear the crap out of everything in sight, so get out of her way!" We talked through our plans on how to get her in the chute. We gritted our teeth as the trailer gates swung open and the rodeo began.

The cow was in a horrible mood because she had been in labor all day. The long labor pains exacerbated the usual bad attitude that she sported on normal days. Surprisingly, she sprang out of the trailer and ran straight to the squeeze chute as if she were ready for help.

After an examination, I discovered the common birthing problem she was battling. She was trying to deliver a breech fetus whose back legs were folded and crossed under his body. He was sitting crisscross-apple sauce in the small uterus. This presentation makes the calf's delivery impossible without help.

The delivery of these cases can be challenging, depending on several factors. Success depends on how cooperative the mom is, how long the calf has been dead, and how much room there is to straighten the legs out. This turned out to be a very challenging deliver.

The legs were crossed and stiff because of rigor mortis in the fetus. The calf had been dead for some time. He was bloated, stiff and stinky. With a couple of epidurals and several breaks to allow the feeling to return to my arms, I could get the first leg pulled into the birth canal. The delivery of the dead calf went quickly from that point on. The entire process still took about an hour, and it covered me with sweat and blood.

The cow was unappreciative, and her mood had not improved at all as we prepared to load her back into the trailer. We double-latched all the gates and planned our escape routes in case the cow did not follow our plan. As feared, the cow did not load into the trailer as well as she had entered the chute.

She rammed every fence, gate and post while blowing snot everywhere. She had no desire to enter the trailer, but wanted a piece of any human in sight. Eric and I flailed our arms and shouted in an attempt to get her to run into the trailer. Our efforts were unsuccessful.

After several attempts and near misses, the cow finally grew tired of our harassment and sprang into the trailer. She moved and leaped well for a cow with a couple of epidurals on board. As per our plan, Eric and I slung the double back gates of the trailer closed. My gate miraculously slammed, rattled and latched all in one motion as I pushed it closed, but Eric wasn't so fortunate.

His gate swung inward too far inside the trailer toward the cow. The opening was just large enough to allow the cow to rush through it. She blew snot on her way to flatten the 6-foot 5-inch, thin-as-a rail cowboy. And flatten the cowboy she did! She laid him flat out on his back and shot through the gap created between the barn door and the trailer.

It was about 11:15 when the cow made her escape, and it was as dark as coal behind the barn. The black cow snorted and contemplated her escape route. I didn't know what to do. My options were to try and coax the cow back into the barn by running like a rodeo clown in front of her as she chased me or to render aid to the pancaked cowboy.

I decided to make sure Eric was still alive and then chase the cow. As I turned to Eric, he was moaning in a whisper and trying to determine which way was up. He sat up slowly and took an inventory of all his body parts. He tried repeatedly to shake the cobwebs out of his head.

The cow did not wait around to see if Eric survived. She was on the lam and sprinted to freedom. I ran out of the barn and stopped for a moment to allow my eyes to adjust to the total darkness. I caught a glimpse of the cow as she ran behind the church next door and headed toward a major highway intersection around the corner.

I slung the cattle prod over my shoulder and gave chase. It wasn't until the cool breeze hit me that I realized the entire front half of my body was covered in blood. Cattle deliveries are messy with fetal fluids and maternal bleeding. Breech deliveries force you to reach into the birth canal to armpit depths, which causes you to be covered in gunk. This delivery was exceeding messy, and I was a covered completely.

As I ran after the cow, I suddenly realized that the cattle prod which was thrown over my shoulder resembled a rifle. I feared a police officer would see me running late in the dark, covered with blood and carrying a "gun". I worried he would have me tackled, cuffed, brutalized and body-cavity searched before I could explain what was going on!

My worst fears almost became a reality when I turned the corner and saw the cow standing in the middle of the intersection while a deputy sheriff sat at the light in his patrol car. He appeared to be rubbing his eyes and trying to determine if what he was seeing was real or the result of a donut sugar rush.

He turned on his patrol lights to warn oncoming traffic of the cow's position. His patrol lights angered the cow even more, and she turned south and headed towards the busy Waterhole 83 Convenience Store. The store is always open and always busy with people. The deputy and I were hot on her trail.

The angry cow sent chills down my spine as she approached the store. I feared she might chase an unsuspecting patron in the front door and demolish the entire inside of our landmark store. I doubted that my insurance would pay for the destruction of an entire Little Debbie Snack section by the crazy cow. These thoughts made me run faster after the cow, shouting at the top of my lungs.

Fortunately, before the cow got to the store, she encountered more cars traveling north down the busy highway and turned back in my direction. As she approached me at a full run, I hoped to turn her into the large, gated yard of the vacant petroleum distribution center by Waterhole 83.

When she got near me, I discovered she was not turning at all. Instead, she still wanted a piece of me and lowered her snot-blowing head in an attempt to lay me out. She charged and grunted loudly. One of us passed gas loudly as the chase began.

She chased me at Mach 5 as I ran for my life. My tactical plan was to circle around the three telephone poles placed in a triangular configuration in front of the old Fronk Oil Company until the cow got tired and quit running. I ran like Carl Lewis because I could hear the cow's bellows near my ears and felt her hot breath on my back. I ran so fast I think I almost lapped the cow. It ended up looking like I was chasing the cow around the telephone poles. We couldn't tell who was chasing who at this point.

She ran faster because she could now hear my bellows and gasps for air near her ears as I chased her. She would have felt my hot breath on her backside if she wasn't still numb from her epidurals. The cow obviously did not understand physics and Newton's Laws of Motion.

This twist of fate confused her profoundly. She ran from me as if I were the crazy one. She darted back onto the highway. Traffic was going in all directions. By this time, the news had spread over the police scanner and people were showing up to witness the excitement.

At this point, I was hoping someone would just run over the cow and put me out of her misery. I couldn't be so lucky. The cow tried to stop abruptly and fell on her side in front of an oncoming car. The red mustang came to a screeching halt just inches from her flailing body.

As she battled to get up, the cow's afterbirth plopped out and landed in the south bound passing lane of Highway 83. Cattle afterbirth is the original "Ooze". It is heavy, gross, slimy and difficult to grip. It's ten times as slippery as a banana peel. The cow looked like she was running on ice as she hopped up and tried to run herself free of the afterbirth pile.

By this time, there were three deputies, me and Eric in pursuit of the cow. She had enough of the city life and headed southeast into the open field. The field was located next to a wealthy housing edition and out of the city limits. She headed straight toward my house about 1 mile southeast of town.

I didn't know if this was a good or a bad thing. I instructed the police officers and Eric to continue heading the cow towards my house while I ran back to the clinic to get a rope and my car. At this point in my career, I did not yet have a tranquilizing dart gun to use on the cow, so we had to hope for the best and try to capture her the old-fashioned way.

As I hustled to return to the chase in my Durango, I called home to warn my wife and kids to stay in the house when they heard the commotion. The cow did not need the added excitement of barking dogs harassing her, so they secured our fat pooches in the garage.

I hoped the cow would see my fat, lazy cow herd when she got to the house and want to join them. I wanted their lethargy to be contagious and wear off on her. The plan was to open the gate as she got near and let her join my tame cow herd and calm down.

I raced home to open the gates before the cow could get there. As I drove south down Highway 83 in the passing lane, my Durango hit the huge wad of afterbirth and the tires spun out. The bloody afterbirth exploded everywhere. It was quite a mess. The blood and slime splattered all over my white Durango and the highway.

While I was hydroplaning across the road, I was glad I wasn't the young motorcycle rider that cruises around town without his helmet. It would have caused a horrific crash on the motorcycle, and he would have slid for miles on the slick afterbirth. He would have looked like a large puddle of afterbirth when he finally slid to a stop. That would be a horrible way to die.

It would definitely be a unique way to go. No one else in the history of humankind would have died that way. I got out of my car to move the mess when I finally stopped. But there was one problem, there was not a piece big enough to pick up. The fetal membranes were pulverized all over the pavement and my car.

I jumped back into my car and rushed home. As I arrived at my house, I saw one deputy standing in front of his car, waving his arms and shouting. He was trying to turn the charging cow towards my pasture. The cow lowered her head, blew snot and ran right smack over him. The blow tested the strength of his bullet-proof vest and sent him rolling down the county road and into the ditch.

He showed remarkable restraint by not unloading his service revolver on the cow. Instead, he got up, dusted himself off, got into his patrol car and went back to the office, followed by the other two deputy's cars. They'd had enough of chasing the cow and figured it was beyond their job descriptions. This left Eric and me all alone to capture the cow.

Like all our other plans, the plan to get her in my pasture did not work well either. We had a difficult time convincing the cow to enter through the gate to join my cattle herd. My wide-eyed cows and obese miniature donkey named Secretariat seemed to be glad.

Perhaps the wild cow was afraid my morbidly obese cattle might eat her. Instead of entering the gate, the cow would charge at me while I held the gate open. I felt like a matador as she whiffed by me time after time. Eric travelled at least 50 miles as he chased the cow up and down the fence line. The amazing thing was the thin cow who had been in labor all day and had received two epidurals was still as energetic as ever. She never seemed to get tired.

After hours of commotion and flashing lights outside his house, my next-door neighbor bravely ventured out of his house to help us get the cow penned. He stood at the opposite end of the fence line as the cow ran by the gate again and headed in his direction. The cow had a full head of steam as she locked in on Keith, who was trying to do the neighborly thing. I yelled to warn him, but it was too late.

The entire event seemed to occur in slow motion as the carnage played out in front of me. The cow lowered her head and went into full ramming mode again as Keith flinched and screamed like a school kid. I also lowered my head because I couldn't bear to watch the demise of my neighbor.

The screeching must have frightened her. She hit him and made a sharp turn to the right. The sharp turn and momentum sent her through the five-strand barbed-wire fence, a two-wire electric fence and into the pasture with my cattle.

My cattle were very excited and showed a burst of energy by running and bucking. My moderately obese donkey even ran, bucked and farted several times. The wild cow stood still and watched the show for a bit before trotting off to join her new mates in the performance. The exercise stopped as I poured out a bucket of cattle cake for the cows to eat and they hustled over to scarf it down.

The wild cow settled in nicely. My cows liked her because they could talk her out of some of her portion of the daily ration. She stayed with my fat cows for a couple of weeks before she calmed down enough to be loaded and hauled home. My cows' lethargy did finally wear off on her because she slowly walked into and off the trailer.

The news of my "Running of the Cow" event traveled through town, as many people followed the chain of events on their police scanners. A local radio personality called to ask if this might have been a "Mad Cow" diagnosis, which had been all over the news. I assured him with a chuckle that, while she was definitely not a "mad cow", she sure was ticked off that night.

RANDY L. SKAGGS, DVM

A Long, Tough Road

There are two things that are certain when local rancher Sam Brillhart calls with a cattle problem. It will be a significant challenge and I will need a full tank of gas in my automobile.

Sam is a very good cowboy and does a lot of his own veterinary jobs. He is a tough man who has only slowed down slightly because of severe back problems over the last few years. He is very skilled at handling many of the large animal veterinary diagnostic and treatment problems.

When he decides it is time to get help, it is a real challenge. Sam developed his skills out of necessity because his father was a rough, old cowboy named James who didn't believe in calling the vet unless the situation was hopeless.

James was the type that would call you to look at a cow that had been down and unable to get up for three days and he'd be very disappointed that the dying cow would not jump up after one quick injection. Like many older ranchers, James never vaccinated his herd against any disease, including the very basic disease of Blackleg. I had never seen an actual case of Blackleg because of common vaccination practices that prevented its occurrence. Almost everyone in the cattle industry gave this basic vaccination.

James did not follow these protocols and lost ten head of adult cows to the disease all in one night. The value of those 10 cows could have bought a lifetime supply of Blackleg vaccine for the Brillhart Ranch. Sam and James learned a tough lesson with that slip-up and Sam became a better manager.

Early one windy spring Texas Panhandle day, Sam called and needed help with a young Angus heifer who was calving. The heifer was on his father's land about 30 miles from my clinic and he couldn't get her up. After loading up the calf delivering equipment, my technician and I were on our way. These long drives are common in rural Texas because the ranches are large, with a lot of miles between them.

These drives give you ample time to ponder current events or get caught up on the news and latest music on the radio. Even though I drove a gas-guzzling SUV, I thought a half tank of gas would be more than enough for the trip. I didn't calculate the extra fuel necessary with a 50-mph wind.

Sam was waiting at the pasture gate in his truck to lead us to the cow. She was deep in the pasture.

The road was extremely rough because of the heavy spring wash-out from the rainstorms and my ride was taking a beating. We kept driving and driving deep into the canyon.

Finally, Sam came to an abrupt stop and jumped out of his truck and hopped in with us to ride the rest of the way. I think he did this to save the wear on his truck, since the roughest part of the ride was yet to come. While we bounced and clanked the rest of the way, Sam explained the heifer was down in a rough canyon and couldn't get up.

It amazed me that Sam even found the heifer because of her isolation. I didn't fully concentrate on the story, as all I could think about was the sound of the mesquite brush scratching the paint on my ride.

We drove as close to the heifer as possible and had to walk the last 100 yards. We struggled to carry the heavy calf puller and toolbox full of medications. Even though Sam assured us the heifer could not get up, I took the halter just in case. Most of the farm visits on 'down cows', which the owner claims cannot get up, actually jump up when they see me coming and run like Carl Lewis.

As we approached this heifer with all our gear and surprised her, her eyes got wide and she jumped up and took off. She was very uncomfortable with her labor pains and went down again. I was able to snag her with the halter. In most pasture situations, I tie the cow's head to her back leg so that she can't get up and take off.

This heifer had her body wedged in a sloping canyon in a deep trough, which made this maneuver impossible. I secured the rope to what looked like a strong mesquite bush and hoped it would outlast the delivery.

The delivery was difficult, as expected. The heifer's pelvis was small, and the calf was breech, with both back legs crossed under his body. This delivery would have been tough, even under ideal conditions. Because of the slope of the canyon and the angle of the heifer, gravity was pulling the calf into the birth canal.

The heifer was too tired to push anymore, which helped. Cows can generate tremendous force inside the pelvis when they're pushing to deliver a calf. The pressure exerted on your arms causes you to lose feeling in your hands and arms during difficult deliveries. During the spring calving season, my arms stay bruised and numb due to this pressure.

Because she was exhausted, the heifer laid still and allowed me to reposition the calf for delivery.

My technician and Sam pushed on the heifer's side to prevent her from rolling over and falling into an even deeper canyon beside her. I grunted and groaned, trying to get the calf repositioned, but without success.

It didn't take long to determine that this approach would not work because the calf was wedged in the birth canal with the help of gravity. Another plan had to be formulated.

Sam and I found a large rock and resorted to Plan B. With as much force as we could muster, we lifted the heifer's rump high enough to slide the rock under her back legs. This allowed the calf to be pushed forward just enough for the legs to be uncrossed and straightened into the birth canal.

With the legs entering the birth canal first, the delivery progressed rapidly. Unfortunately, the calf was dead. The status of her calf didn't seem to matter to the heifer. She was not sticking around to check on him. As the calf exited her body and hit the ground, she sprang to her feet, uprooted the mesquite bush and took off like we shot her out of a cannon.

It was comical seeing the cow wearing the red halter and dragging the large, up-rooted mesquite bush as she sprinted out of the canyon. Since she was about 100 pounds lighter, she could really move. If she were not unsteady on her back legs from the epidural, she might have set an over-land speed record. The birthing team looked at each other, wondering what had just occurred.

The chain of events happened so rapidly that it left us a little foggy with our eyes watering. It may have just been the dust and birthing fluids the fleeing cow kicked in our eyes. Either way, it was a memorable moment.

The hike back to the car seemed even longer as we struggled to carry the blood-soaked equipment while wearing our muddy, damp clothes. We threw the stuff in the back hatch of the SUV with no regard for what splattered where and began the long drive home.

Up to this point, my luck had not been all that good. As it turned out, my luck got better this day and ended up being all good. Just as I made it back to town, the low fuel alarm on my dash began chirping as my engine sputtered. I coasted into the station just before the engine died.

It worked out perfectly. It sure would have been a long walk back to town if I had run out of gas in the country. No one in their right mind would have stopped to pick up a blood-stained man on a lonely country road.

Several weeks later, Sam returned the red halter. It was much worse for wear, with mesquite thorns imbedded in the knotted and frayed rope. It had faded from bright red to a light pink color. I'm sure the story of how Sam got it off the cow was a good one.

Doctor #207731 From Cell Block 3

The four years I spent studying at vet school were full of stress and pressure. Despite the tension, these years also created many fond memories for me.

As the curriculum progressed into the fourth year, there were a few rotations that offered a chance to relax a little and perform many of the tasks that veterinarians do daily. The rotations that allowed us to work on the animals belonging to the Texas Department of Corrections were hands-on and stress-free.

The prison system in Texas is totally self-sustaining in food production. They raise all the animals and crops needed to feed the inmates. The Texas A&M vet school provided many of the animal care services for them free of charge.

This arrangement was beneficial to both entities due to experience gained by the students and low cost for the prison system. As a result, there were many opportunities for students to gain valuable experience and tackle many different animal issues.

The prison rotations were not all stress-free. Entering the prisons was disturbing to those of us who had led sheltered childhoods. The confinement and the feeling of risk were palpable to me. The vet students were prepared before the rotations began. They informed us to remove our name tags and not give out any personal information to any of the prisoners or trustees.

We were briefed on what behavior to have, even though we seldom ever had contact with dangerous criminals. We never worked with the hardened criminals but were assisted by the very low risk trustees. Despite knowing this, it was still scary to sign the "no negotiation for hostages" clause before entering the prison grounds.

The highest risk rotation for the students had nothing to do with the inmates. It was the prison horse farm rotation. Most of the horses that were treated were well mannered and behaved just like most of the trustees. The procedures performed on the mild-mannered horses included de-worming, vaccinating, suturing and treating mild illnesses.

But the young colts in the stud pen were a lot like the inmates in the maximum security section of the penitentiary. None of the colts in the castration section were mild-mannered. These horses were young, wild, and crazy. Most of them had never seen a human who was not wearing a black-and-white striped outfit. In fact, they had very little human interaction until the day they sent us to castrate them.

This rotation also exposed us to the prisoners who were the most dangerous. These inmates were not trustees and had signed up for this dangerous duty, hoping to get some fresh air and getting banged up a bit. If they were injured, they got to spend a few days at the infirmary, resting and healing. They were like the colts and were ready to charge full steam ahead.

The castration process was a group effort by all the students on the rotation. Some students were to anesthetize the frightened colt, while others took part in the castration procedure. Each student did each of the different duties. All fifteen of the nervous colts were in one large lot, which was probably two acres in size.

Two older prisoners would approach the group and try to isolate the next patient. Once they separated a colt out of the pack, several inmates would bull rush him and wrestle the 900-colt to the ground.

Once the dust cleared and the colt was subdued, the students would run in and attempt to give the anesthesia in the horse's jugular vein. Giving the IV injection wasn't easy at that stage of our careers and it was made more challenging because we had to dodge the flying hooves and thrashing head. It was more like a rodeo event rather than medicine.

The simple part of the entire process was the surgery itself. Despite being puckered because it was my first horse castration, I didn't have to worry because I knew they securely held the horse. That might have been the only thing I felt secure about around those inmates. The guards made sure the prisoners provided all the muscle and absorbed most of the trauma. These prisoners were loaded with brawn and low on brains.

On the opposite end of the spectrum, the trustees who were assigned to caring for the cattle herds were the most intelligent and trusted prisoners. They were often well educated and well trained. Most of these men had been in the system for an extended period and required minimal supervision.

Yearly maintenance for the cows in the prison's herd was a group effort. Each cow was pushed into the chute by the trustees and then checked from head to toe by the students. Veterinary students performed pregnancy tests, vaccinated, dewormed, checked hooves, horns and udders, and took blood samples to test for Brucellosis.

In the outside-world, the blood sample for this test is usually taken from the tail vein because of easy access and convenience. That was not the case with these cattle. This sample was taken from the large jugular vein in the neck because the cow was getting pregnancy tested on the other end by a student and clinician. The trustee would nose-clamp the cow and pull her head to one side.

The entire process moved quickly because there were thousands of cows to be processed. The students rotated and took turns doing the different duties. I was nervous because it was my first time to draw a blood sample from a cow's jugular vein. Nonetheless, I tried to charge in with confidence once the trustee secured the head.

I dropped on my right knee and put pressure on the base of the cow's neck with my left hand, just as they had instructed us to do. This pressure causes the large vein to distend with blood and becomes easily seen in most cases. It was summer, so there was no excessive hair to make the job more difficult. I felt like things were going in my favor. I identified the anatomical landmarks and took a shot at the vein.

I jabbed the 16-gauge needle through the tough skin on the cow's neck and began the "jab and suck" method with the syringe. I advanced the needle back and forth and side to side hoping to see the dark red fluid gush into the syringe.

To my despair, the syringe remained empty. I felt the sweat building up on my forehead and my muscles tense up. The time seemed to pass quickly, and I felt that frantic feeling building up. It terrified me I might be the last one done on this cow and have to endure the verbal abuse of my classmates and instructors.

I continued to jab and poke to no avail. Just when I thought all was lost, I felt a couple of strong thumps on my left shoulder. I looked up, expecting to see the disgusted instructor. Instead, it was the old trustee who was holding the cow's head.

He smiled and said, "Hey man, try right here!".

He pointed to the huge vein with his finger, which was about 3 inches from where I had been fishing. Sure enough, I struck blood when I inserted the needle into the large vein that he had pointed out. It was the size of a garden hose.

The trustee chuckled and said, "Don't feel bad, Doc! It happens all the time, man. 'Cause they got you guys all way too puckered! Ya's gotta relax."

Puckered I was. The pucker relaxed a little after I hit the vein and got the sample. With the trustee's help, I did pretty well with the rest of the samples. Since that day, each time I draw blood from a cow's jugular vein, I remember that trustee. He is probably still at the prison, training tomorrow's veterinarians on the art of hitting jugular veins.

Would the Real "Curly" Step Forward?

In rural parts of the country, veterinarians are often expected to do cowboy work. The work involves helping round up and pen the sick animal or doing the yearly processing of the herd. Some cattle owners do not enjoy the hands-on experience of processing their cattle, so they call for help.

Processing or "working" cattle involves branding, castrating or banding, vaccinating, de-horning and de-worming the cattle. This is at least a yearly event and primarily involves processing the calf crop for that year.

As the years pass, it seems like more and more people do not want to process their own cattle. Most of my clients have found people to do that for them, but a few still have me do this loud, messy and smelly duty. The older I get, the less I enjoy it. The clinic staff really doesn't enjoy the mess.

Some of my favorite ranchers who have me process their cattle are a couple of older female clients. They love their cattle and watch them carefully. The cattle are a hobby for the couple.

Neither of them spends much of their enormous fortunes on creature comforts for themselves, but they spare no expense in caring for their cattle. Most of their cows are pets, have names, and are registered. They pamper the females but seem to care a little less about the bulls. They bring expecting-cows to the clinic during snowstorms to keep them out of the cold weather and have her calves inside the heated barn.

The ladies prefer to drop the cattle off at the clinic to be processed with specific instructions. They never stick around to help because they can't stand to see the animals in any discomfort. The younger lady always leaves a note in the barn near the chute with specific instructions.

The list includes the ear-tag number of the calves she thinks need an antibiotic shot, which ones need to be branded or vaccinated differently and ones that need a specific tattoo. The purebred, registered bulls and heifers require a special tattoo placed in their ear for registration.

Cindy's lists are usually excellent, with all the needed information, but sometimes the list is less than complete and is confusing. One such time, she had a list of the three bulls out of the 30 head of calves that she wanted to keep for breeding bulls.

The calves would be processed, but the castration procedure would be skipped. This was excellent news for those three lucky bulls. They would not be turned into T-bone steaks soon, and their sole job would be to impregnate all the heifers.

Most of their calves already had tags in their ears. Cindy and Claire tried to catch the babies at birth and tag them. Occasionally, the cows did not allow that, so we had to tag them during processing. Since the calves were purebred Black Angus, they all looked similar and needed some form of identification to tell help them apart.

As I looked over Cindy's long, crumpled list of instructions written on an old piece of paper feed bag, I noticed a problem. Under the heading of "3 calves to be left as bulls" was the list - #12, # 23 and Curly. I looked at the large group of cattle and didn't see any particular bull calf that looked like a "Curly". It stumped me.

My technician laughed as I paged Curly as if on an intercom, "Curly, Curly, CURLY…… would the real Curly please come forward."

The cattle and my technician looked at me like I had lost my mind and no volunteers stepped forward. It would have been a great opportunity for one bull that was not Curly. He could have stepped out and saved his manhood, but no one seized the moment.

I called Cindy who tried to shed some light on the list. "Curly is the black bull with the curly swatch of hair on his forehead!" she explained. This tidbit helped in no way.

I walked through the wave of black cattle again but observed no curly swatches. Maybe his hair had been tussled in the trailer. I was still clueless, but amused by her identification system.

I finally had to have Cindy come back and point him out. She got a much better response than I did. As soon as she arrived, she walked into the barn and yelled, "Curly!" A bull with a curly swatch of hair appeared from the center of the mass of cattle to answer her call.

The swatch of tussled hair was so obvious at that point. He looked just like a Curly. I couldn't believe he didn't respond to my call, but I bet his mom and Cindy had taught him not to talk to strangers.

Part Four:
Horses and Mules

RANDY L. SKAGGS, DVM

Snake Charming and Horse Wrangling in the Dark of Night

Some nights in the rural parts of the Texas Panhandle are pitch black. So dark, in fact, that you have a difficult time seeing your own hand when it's held right in front of your face. The sky is black and expansive. Stars twinkle faintly, like fireflies in the distance. The land is flat and there are few city lights and no tall buildings to obstruct your view.

The darkness is great for gazing at the stars and telling scary campfire stories. It makes other jobs impossible. Finding a totally black colt that needs medical attention is tough and one of those jobs.

The late-night call sent me to the Lake Fryer area to render aid to a young colt that had been the victim of a rattlesnake bite. The Lake Fryer region seems darker than other areas because it sits in a small canyon with many trees. Trees are a scarce commodity in the Texas Panhandle, and the Lake Fryer area has more than its fair share.

Many of these are old, majestic Cottonwood trees that have battled the harsh environment for years. They have survived droughts, insects and fires to grow very large. But, as with all soft wooded trees, they are prone to losing dead limbs in the strong winds. The limbs are tripping hazards and shin busters as they collect around the enormous tree trunks.

As is often the case with horses, the irritable rattlesnake had struck this young colt on the nose. Horses are curious creatures and like to sniff and get a close look at the coiled rattlesnakes. This curiosity gives the snake an easy opportunity and target. The snakes sink their fangs into the tissue and inject a nasty toxin. They often deposit opportunistic bacteria that thrive on the damaged tissues as well.

The venom is very reactive and causes acute pain and significant swelling once it enters the tissues. The swelling is profuse, rapid, and can be life threatening if it occludes the horse's airways.

If the swelling and reaction to the venom does not kill the horse, it is common for them to get a severe infection at the site of the bite. This infection can also be hard to control and can become fatal. As a result, it is important to begin therapy as soon as possible to increase the odds of treatment success.

This colt was not making the treatment task easy. He was scared and did not yet trust people. His registered name was Buster's Last Stand. His geriatric father, named "Buster", was a long-time resident of the farm.

The old lethargic Buster mustered up enough energy one sunny spring day to mount and mate with a willing mare. He gave the mating effort his all and dropped dead immediately after the dismount. The sexual act zapped every last bit of life out of old Buster. As a result, the conceived colt was officially named Buster's Last Stand, or BLS, in memory of the event.

We had no functional flashlights to use in finding the colt, which was ridiculous and made the job much more difficult. My usually dependable flashlight was dead as a doornail.

We parked our trucks at the entrance to the pasture and shined the lights on the bright setting to pierce through the pitch-black night. Because of the large trees and undulating terrain, it helped little. In fact, the lights only served the purpose of blinding you when you glanced in their direction.

We could hear the constricted, labored respiratory efforts of the colt when we entered the 20-acre trap, but the sound was difficult to pick up because of the ruffling of the cottonwood trees in the Texas breeze. We stumbled around the pasture, looking, listening, and feeling for the colt.

My fear was that I would surprise the horse in the dark and touch his hindquarters. The unexpected touch would cause the terrified horse to respond with a swift kick in my general direction. Horse kicks are fast and powerful. If on target, the kick would inflict great pain and could be lethal.

As we made our way into the heart of the pasture, I suddenly realized that the field also contained the rattlesnake or snakes that had caused the problem. This made me very uneasy. I dislike any snake that is not on my exam table. While I do not mind treating them at the office, I detest being surprised by the slippery creatures in the wild.

I went into a ridiculous-looking, high stepping, anti-snake gait. I tried to stay in the middle of the pack of horse hunters. I figured people on the outside of the pack would be more likely snake bit. My focus turned less on listening for the sound of a horse's labored breathing and targeted more at detecting the frightening sound of a rattling snake tail.

The pasture was filled with the fallen limbs of the old, majestic cottonwood trees and tall weeds which brushed against my legs. This added to my apprehension. Despite the adversities, the brave group charged on, hoping to find the colt and save his life.

As we combed the pasture near a cluster of trees, our braveness evaporated into thin air when the distinct sounds of an angry snake rattled in the air.

Childish screams of "snake", "run" and "look out" came mainly from me and pierced the calm night. We ran like track stars toward the truck lights. We sprinted like our pants were on fire and scurried towards the light.

I don't know if it was the sound of the snake or the sound of the shrieking rescuers that frighten the colt into running for the lights as well. While it seemed like we were running at a 100 miles per hour, we were still no match for the young colt. He was standing calmly near the trucks at the gate when we got there. While we coughed, panted and gasp for air, the colt breathed at a normal rate, although his nose was two times its normal size.

Once my breathing returned to normal and my eyes stopped watering, I could see that the swelling in the colt's face was not as bad as most. The fang marks and draining blood on the bridge of his nose were about 1 1/2 inches apart. The large space between fang marks showed the snake was a very large one.

It looked like the colt had taken a direct hit. The limited extent of the damage meant that the snake must have recently bitten something before striking the colt. The swelling was relatively minimal and was not life-threatening.

It takes time between strikes for the venom to be replaced by the snake, which is why it is better to be the second person in the group to be bitten. The minimal swelling meant that the colt would not need a tracheotomy to breathe. He could be treated much more conservative, with shots of an antibiotic, an anti-inflammatory and an anti-venom.

The treatment was successful, and the colt healed uneventfully. As usual, the swelling slowly regressed over the next few days and the antibiotic kept the infection in check.

After I had treated the horse, the crowd drove down to the cluster of trees to hunt for the snake. The group's bravery had returned, and they had renewed strength in numbers. My bravery was gone, and I wanted no part of this dangerous event.

They armed themselves with shovels and hoes. In my mind, there is no shovel or hoe handle long enough to keep me safe. The crowd snooped in all the cracks and crevices around the trees where the snakes could hide. The adventurous mob ended up being successful. A report the next day revealed that the group ended up killing three snakes in the cluster of cottonwood trees. The snakes were large, ornery, and aggressive.

On my long drive home, I decided I should take up a new hobby. Star gazing sounded much safer in the pitch-dark Panhandle nights than horse wrangling and snake charming.

Horse Castration: The Spectator's Sport

One hot and dry August day, I made the trip down to the Lake Fryer area just south of Perryton to castrate a horse. It was about 25 miles from my office, so I had ample time to survey the damage brought on by the severe summer drought. There were cracks in the soil that small children and dogs could fall into and never be heard from or seen again.

The grass and trees were brown and parched because of many consecutive days of 100-degree heat. The high heat was also taking its toll on pets and people. I found myself grumpier and shorter fused than ever. The normally scenic, pleasant drive seemed much longer than usual in the heat. The pasture cattle crowded together under the sparse trees, yearning for shade and relief from the heat. They only grazed during the cool morning and evening hours.

Since the drive was not its usual attention-grabber, I reflected on the many meanings of the phrase "halter broke colt". This phrase's definition would take several pages in the cowboy dictionary because everyone has their own definition and description of "halter broke". There is not a steadfast definition for "halter broke colt".

In most veterinarians' dreams, "halter broke" is defined as a gentle, easy-going colt standing under a well-padded, cool shade tree while flipping his lead rope up so you don't have to bend over to pick it up.

In the horse trainer's world, "halter broke" means the colt has seen a halter without pawing and kicking at anything that moves. As I found out on this day, a would-be horse trainer (who was also a preacher and friend of the colt owner) had a very different definition of "halter broke".

Apparently, his definition of "halter broke" was a colt that had seen a halter for the second time without totally freaking out. The first time this colt observed a halter, he cleared the 6-foot fence and waved goodbye with his nappy-haired tail.

As I pulled up, I knew the colt would be apprehensive because of the extremely large number of family members and co-owners that showed up to witness the event. Each co-owner was well equipped with video and traditional cameras, which they had been firing repeatedly to capture every step of the event.

They had been snapping pictures right and left for several minutes before my arrival, and the horse's eyes were as big as saucers. He seemed frustrated, and a little chapped.

The group of co-owners included several middle-aged brothers and cousins, as well as their aging fathers. They were all members of the Ellzey family, which were long-time residents of Ochiltree County and played heavily in its history and character. The group was in high spirits and seemed to enjoy each other's company.

The lone female of the group was a sister who was all tomboy and held her own with little effort. Jill was actually the most helpful member of the entourage. She was a seasoned first-grade teacher and had patience. She was the only one in the group that paid attention and was reliable help.

The crowd's conversation was very loud, and everyone seemed to enjoy life. On the other hand, the wiry, dull-haired colt wasn't sharing their vigor for the event. The noise irritated the inherently nervous colt.

The colt was very shaken by the time I unloaded my equipment and entered his lot. He was an odd-looking colt that had a very short, frayed tail. He probably weighed about 600 pounds, but was very athletic. I chased him around the lot for 30 minutes with the preacher chanting horse-whisperer commands to him.

The preacher might as well as have been speaking in tongues because it had no calming effect on the horse. He should have yelled the whispered commands because the colt obviously could not hear them. I felt very tense in the hot temperature and was at a significant disadvantage.

Because of my proximity to a man of God, I had to concentrate on suppressing my desire to yell obscenities at the crazy colt. As time went on, I hoped that the batteries on the video cameras would wear down before we started the surgery on the colt, and before someone got maimed. Video documentation usually causes anything that can go wrong to go wrong.

As time went by, the fractious colt would let me get just close to catching him, so he could have another attempt at pawing my head. Just before I started horse-whispering in tongues to this devil-possessed colt, the heat took its toll and the colt admitted defeat. He allowed me to grab and hold on to his halter.

As it turned out, catching the colt was the simple part of the process. The real difficulty came with administering the anesthesia. Horses are castrated under general anesthesia, which involves giving them a tranquilizer by intravenous injection before inducing a surgical plane of anesthesia with another intravenous injection. The colt put up a fight and was not interested in getting the first shot.

I had to resort to giving the injection in the muscle instead of the vein, which delays the effect. As sometimes occurs in anesthesia of already excited horses, the colt was not affected by the first tranquilizer and required a second. The second dose of Xylazine worked only slightly better than the first, but the horse became almost manageable instead of stumbling-drunk like most colts.

As I approached the colt to give the general anesthetic injection, I not only had to concentrate on hitting the vein, but also had to provide commentary to the crowd. I explain how the new anesthetic and surgical techniques were better than the previous decade's techniques.

Despite the distractions, the Ketamine injection went off without a hitch. The crowd sensed the approaching excitement of the horse going down and followed my request to clear the lot before the horse fell on them.

Slowly but surely, the horse fell to his side as I guided him to fall on his left side. Having the horse on his left side is preferred by right-handed surgeons because it is easier to retract the testicles and make the scrotal incision. Despite my best efforts, the horse went down in the only sunny spot in the entire lot. This was perfect for video and photography documentation, but boiling on the surgeon.

The technician and I moved at our usual rapid pace to pad the horse's head, cover his eyes and secure a rope to hold his up sided back leg. The rope on the back leg helps by allowing the leg to be pulled forward and clear of the surgery site. Its main purpose, though, is to prevent the surgeon from getting the snot kicked out of him during the initial incision. If the patient is not quite at a surgical plane of anesthesia, that can happen.

The anesthetic time ranges from 10 to 15 minutes, which necessitates a swift attack. Once the crowd felt the horse was safely under anesthesia, they packed back into the lot. I felt like an athlete running an obstacle course. I scurried around the spectators, carrying the bucket full of surgical instruments and scrub, and packing the tetanus injections and antibiotic shot in my chest pocket.

The crowd seemed oblivious to my struggle as they jockeyed to get the best spot to view and film the horse castration. They backed up only slightly as I warned them that the horse might still kick with the initial incision. The men laughed nervously as I said it had been some time since I had castrated the wrong patient in a crowd this size.

The cameras clicked and the video lights blazed as I approached the horse for the surgery. When it began, it became obvious that what the horse did not have in physical size, he more than made up for in testicular girth. Since I enjoy my work and talking about it, I accommodated the request for a narrative description as the surgery progressed.

I ignored the high risk of having my mouth open since body fluids and feces are likely to fly any time you are working on large animals. I surgically scrubbed the scrotum while giving the brief schedule of events. The schedule went astray quickly.

As my luck would have it, the initial scrotal incision sent a blast of blood (at least I tell myself it was blood) rocketing across my face and into my open mouth. Half the group gasped in horror and the other half felt the need to tease me about my misfortune. I informed the crowd I prefer that my horse fries are battered, covered in Ranch Dressing and a little less fresh. The rest of the castration procedure passed unremarkable, with only one person feeling faint.

Legend has it that if the testicles are thrown behind the colt after the surgery, he will make a good cutting horse. If thrown in front, they will produce a good racehorse, since he will race forward to catch up with his severed parts. The group conferred and decided they preferred a cutting horse rather than a racehorse, so I complied. The fact that I acknowledged this old folk story seemed to delight the aged division of the crowd and improved my credibility.

The younger group made sure that I showed them the removed "Squealer Buttons" to prevent a "proud-cut stud". These structures are part of the sperm delivery tubules of the testicles and produce small amounts of the male hormone testosterone. If these tubules are not removed, the horses will often act like a stud horse after castration. These horses are referred to as "proud-cut horses" and can be a real pain to deal with because they remain very aggressive.

Despite the rough start, the rest of the surgery went well. The colt that didn't want to go to sleep for surgery was in no hurry to awaken, either. My technician noticed my worried demeanor as the colt slept and slept. Usually, the colt is standing up within 10 minutes of the surgery's completion, but this colt did not move for 30 minutes. These 30-minutes seemed extremely long.

The older men in the group asked questions about what would happen now to the glands that helped make up the rest of the horse's reproductive fluids. Undoubtedly, these questions resulted from their own medical problems. This conversation sparked a detailed description of the common prostate problem the older men were having. A few wondered aloud if this surgery would help them overcome their prostate problems. I assumed they were joking.

I'm not sure if it was Divine Intervention or that the entire episode was approaching the length of a feature film, but the colt sprang to his feet with the same exuberance that he had shown initially. He shook his head to clear the cobwebs, sent the audience running, and jumped the fence.

Million-dollar Mule

Almost daily in the veterinary profession, you get to do something unusual. It keeps the job interesting and broadens your horizons.

Bob called one morning with an unusual request. He had a pet mule who ran with his cattle to ward off coyotes. Adult male mules and donkeys, like human adult males, are often very hard to live with. They cause trouble and get into fights with any taker. This mule was becoming too obnoxious and needed "to lose his bawls" according to Bob.

Since most of Bob's animals are on the fractious side, I was frightened by the prospect of working on one that he found obnoxious. None the less, we set up a time for the surgical castration later in the week. I was also a little apprehensive because it had been a while since I had castrated a mule.

Mules are seldom castrated since they are the infertile offspring of a mating between a jackass and a horse. They are very strong-willed and persistent. Mules only do what they want, when

COUNTRY VET

they want, which makes handling them unpredictable.

Bob and his mule were late for their appointment, which disrupted an already hectic day. Bob's grandson, Clayton, came into the clinic to let me know they'd had a little trouble getting the unbroken mule haltered and loaded. This meant the mule was going to be agitated before we began.

When the pair finally showed up, they were both excited and breathing hard. Bob ordered Clayton into the trailer to push the mule out. The mule was a yearling and stood only about 4 feet tall, but was extremely obese because of its easy, sedentary lifestyle. After a lot of grunting and groaning, Clayton pushed the mule out of the trailer into the sand-filled barn. The mule made a loud thump as he landed.

The anesthesia protocol I use in equines requires two shots given several minutes apart, directly in the animal's jugular vein. While I was drawing up the first injection, Clayton decided to prove to his grandfather that he could throw the mule on his side like he would a calf that was to be castrated.

Even though Clayton was a big fella at about 6 feet and 250 pounds, he didn't get close to pitching the mule. The mule was thick and round, with a low center of gravity, just like Bob.

This spectacle made the thick, round Bob laugh so hard that he started coughing and gagging. He couldn't catch his breath. I thought we might need to render CPR before he finally sat down and gasp a few good breaths.

Despite my objections, Bob convinced Clayton to try to ride the mule bareback around the barn a few times. Clayton needed little encouragement and jumped on the mules back with vigor. Because of Clayton's excessive weight, the mule did not feel like making any laps around the barn and stood still.

Bob decided to help and yelled for Clayton to hold on. Bob poked the stubborn mule in the butt with an electric hotshot used on cattle. The mule suddenly felt like taking several rapid laps around the barn while bucking, kicking and breaking wind.

Clayton's loud swearing and howling did nothing to calm the mule's nerves as he pitched and bucked like a rodeo horse. With a hard thud and an enormous cloud of dust, Clayton hit the ground. He landed as softly as a 250-pound man could.

Clayton moaned, groaned and dusted himself off as he limped over to the mule just in time for the real rodeo to begin. I approached the mule with the first tranquillizer injection and realized the mule's neck was as thick as a tree stump. Finding the jugular vein would not be easy. After several attempts at hitting the target with the mule bucking and kicking, I admitted defeat and went to Plan B.

Plan B involved giving the sedative in the muscle and waiting much longer for it to take effect. Plan B was better at saving our toes, shins, and heads from the bucking mule's hooves.

During the wait for the sedative to go to work, Bob told us how much the entire family thought of this mule, which they had named Bronco Buster. Buster was actually a family pet, highly regarded even though he wasn't worth anything. Bob hoped out loud that nothing would happen to his old buddy while he was under anesthesia because he liked him so much.

The sedative finally did its job, and Buster was feeling no pain. The sedative allowed me to take a 2-inch needle and hit the jugular vein with a general anesthetic and induce a surgical state of anesthesia, or so I thought. Apparently, Buster had a very high tolerance to the anesthetic medication. It was two shots later that Buster went to sleep.

The surgery went very well except for the large pockets of fat that packed Buster's scrotum. These pockets dwarfed the small testicles that I was removing. The clumps of fat were a big nuisance because of their very large blood supply. They continually got into the surgical field.

After castration, I gave Bob the option of owning a race mule or a cutting mule. This was a most tough decision for Bob because he didn't know which was more valuable or useful. After a little thought, Bob decided he needed a racing mule, and the testicles were placed accordingly.

Anesthetic recovery was uneventful, and the mule was standing in no time. Bob and Clayton went to the neighboring convenient store to get some refreshments to treat their dehydration while waiting for Buster to wake up enough to go home.

The mule was very reluctant to enter the trailer when they came to pick him up. He wanted no part of getting back into that trailer and fought the entire time. Unfortunately, the fight to get Buster in the trailer caused the fat pockets to bleed somewhat profusely.

While the blood loss wasn't excessive, it looked concerning. To be safe rather than sorry, I kept Buster over-night and monitor him closely. This decision made Bob rest a little easier.

We unloaded Buster and applied a pressure wrap in a diaper configuration to help stop the bleeding. I think the mule was less concerned with being castrated than the risk of having another mule see him wearing a diaper. Buster put up quite a fight and crushed our toes once again as we applied the diaper.

Bob's concern was obvious as he was leaving. "I hope my $500.00 racing mule doesn't die! Call me tonight and let me know how he's doing."

Since I am an excessive worrier, Buster and I spent a lot of time together that night. The bleeding stopped a few minutes after we left him alone and did not return all night. I called Bob's wife to let her know Buster was fine. It relieved her to hear the good news since Bob told her the mule was probably going to "die at the vet's office."

Bob's wife just knew we had castrated her $1,000.00 racing mule at the wrong sign in the Farmer's Almanac and that was what had caused the fat to bleed. I didn't tell her that my old veterinary boss used to castrate by the "signs" as well. The signs were always right no matter what the date was because he castrated by the "dollar signs". The signs were always right for him.

Through the night, I checked on him every two hours. The bleeding never returned, and he did well except for a little lost sleep.

When Bob came to pick him up the next morning, he was glad to see that all had gone well through the night. He said with a large belly laugh, "I'm glad we're not going to have to turn this $1,500.00 racing mule claim over to your insurance agency for collection on a death loss."

It is a good thing that veterinarians treat all the animals like a million dollars because it is hard to tell a valuable racing mule from a pasture pet mule until problems arise. I was glad that Buster went home when he did. By the end of the week, Old Buster would have been worth over two million bucks.

Part Five:
Animals and Their Owners

RANDY L. SKAGGS, DVM

Rest In Peace Unless the Cat Wakes Up

Some requests are so unique that they give a glimpse into the strangeness of apparently normal clients. Mr. Lang was a feeble man who appeared to be near death from the first time I met him several years earlier. Like all the people and animals in his house, he coughed constantly and was on oxygen because of his years of smoking.

Each breath he took was labored and exaggerated from the years of abuse he dished out to his lungs by smoking. The second-hand smoke took its toll on everyone in the house. His wife, son, two dogs and old cat all had the same chronic smoker's cough.

Even when he was forced to be on oxygen, he continued to smoke. He smoked like a chimney despite the risk of causing the oxygen bottle to explode from the cigarette. His need to smoke was more important to him than protecting his family or health.

His two Chinese Pug dogs were identical to Mr. and Mrs. Lang, except they were much more obese than their owners. The Lang's were thin as a rail because of their airway issues and smoking. The dogs were fat and happy but hacked, wheezed, and coughed constantly.

Because of their living conditions, they required frequent trips to my office for upper respiratory tract infections and allergies. They always acted happy to see me, but I think they were just happy to be out of the smoke-filled house.

Mr. Lang's cat, on the other hand, was old, wild and never happy to see me. I did not see him much because of his aggression. He was so wild and hard to handle that I often just sent medicine home for him. On the rare occasion when I examined him, the Lang's son brought the cat in a heavily reinforced cage.

The cage was encircled with duct tape in several places to keep it together. The cat would hiss and growl as he tested the bolts holding the cage together. Exams were quick and often less than thorough in order to save everyone's fingers. The family reported that the cat only liked Mr. Lang. I think the cat just tolerated him.

As the years passed, Mr. Lang finally succumbed to his lifetime of smoking and emphysema. His lungs failed, and he passed away in his 70s. The last few years of his life were spent totally inside his small house with his wife and pets as his companions. The lifetime of smoking had not only shortened his life, but made his last few years miserable.

We were sad but not surprised to hear of Mr. Lang's passing when his wife dropped by the office to make a request. She followed me to the privacy of my office, lugging her oxygen tank and heavy purse. She was sad, very frail and struggling to breathe. The heavy weight of her sorrow showed on her weak body and sad, pale face. I could barely hear her faint whispers and struggled to make sense of what she was muttering.

I leaned in to hear as she whispered, "My husband passed away and he had a last request. His favorite companion and only long-term friend was that old cat. As you know, his cat has not been in good health and he is taking the death of my husband very hard. My husband's request was to have his cat put to sleep when he died and to have him buried with him in his casket. So…… I need you to do that for me."

She whispered with long breaks between phrases in order to get her oxygen level up.

I didn't know what to say, but knew better than to argue or make other suggestions. Once an owner comes to this decision, there is no changing their mind. Since the cat was ancient and had been very ill, it made the process much easier.

I couldn't help but wonder if it wasn't his request at all to be buried with the wild cat. Instead, I wondered if it was the decision of the family, since no one else wanted or liked the cat. It didn't seem reasonable to me he would want this irritable feline in his casket for eternity.

While many families have requested that their loved one's animals be put to sleep after they had passed, I'd never had one that was going to be buried with the owner. Nonetheless, I agreed to put the cat down if she would bring it in several hours before the funeral.

***

About an hour before the funeral was to begin, the son brought the wild cat to the office. The cat was in his typical aggressive and angry mood but did not feel well enough to shred the cage this time. He attacked the door each time I approached the cage. There was no way of getting the furry ball of fire out of the carrier without the risk of losing life and limb.

I put the cat under anesthesia by injection with a 4-foot-long injection pole through the cage door. After several minutes, the old, angry, ill cat was very sleepy. The anesthetic called Ketamine is commonly used for minor surgery and sedation in cats. It served its purpose well in this case. The cat was as limp as a noodle and easily handled in just a few minutes.

Euthanasia in animals is usually a quick and painless process. We inject an extremely high concentration of a barbiturate drug into a large vein. The highly concentrated drug travels quickly to the heart and brain to shut down breathing and heart beats almost instantly. The animals pass in just a few heartbeats.

The drugs work so fast that it can be dangerous at times. Great care must be taken when putting horses to sleep because the drugs can work so fast that the horse will fall on you. The horses can die on the needle before you can get it removed. About three ounces of the thick injection must be given to horses. That volume requires the use of two syringes and more time to complete the injection. Because of the fact that each horse requires a different amount, it makes the last few seconds of the injection kind of dicey.

Unfortunately, not all animals go to sleep so easily. Extremely old and ill patients can create problems. Their veins are fragile and difficult to hit. If the peripheral veins can't be found, the second technique is to inject the medication directly into the heart.

This can also be a challenge in old or ill patients because the heart is small and evasive. It is not uncommon to use two or three times more medication than usual to put these patients to sleep because of vein and heart misses.

Such was the case with Mr. Lang's cat. I could not hit a vein at all. The process seemed to take forever. I worried the service would begin before I could get the cat put to sleep. Or, worse yet, the son would run in after the service began with the ill-tempered, unwanted cat and throw its dead, limp, lifeless body into the casket with his father.

The usual amount of the solution needed to put a cat to sleep is 2 cc. I used 20 cc in this cat to make sure the effort would be successful. I double- and triple-checked for heart beats, pulses and corneal reflexes to be sure the cat was dead. There would be nothing worse than having the cat wake up halfway through the service and begin howling, scratching and destroying the interior of the casket.

Adding to my fears was the fact that I had seen an animal that was apparently euthanized wake up a few hours afterward. In my final year of vet school, I was on the pathology rotation when a horse was put to sleep by the morning surgical rotation. When we opened the cooler door to do a necropsy on the animal after lunch, he was standing there greeting us. Obviously, the surgical students had not done their job well.

It would have been physically and emotionally traumatic for those at the service if the cat had awakened. I'm sure the casket was not reinforced with duct tape and the cat would have been out of that thing in no time. The cat would have a lot of easy prey to abuse. None of the family could have run far or fast because of their second-hand lung disease.

The preacher would have needed a pole injector loaded with Ketamine to restore order and finish the service.

One Last Favor

I love my job. After 30 years of daily practice, there are still "firsts" on many occasions. Some of these new experiences are unpleasant, but most are enjoyable and liven up the day. They help break up the monotony that sometimes consumes our daily schedule.

Farm visits are a common occurrence in rural veterinary practices. These trips can be long or short, boring or exciting, and often frustrating. The travel takes time away from doing something much more interesting. Almost all the farm visits involve the treatment of farm animals.

It's very rare to make a farm visit specifically to treat a dog or cat. Occasionally, the small animals running around the farm get looked at or vaccinated after we finish treating the valuable horses and cattle.

On rare occasions, I've visited farms to put down a farmer's favorite old dog. These dogs have to be very special. They are the farmer's favorite pet which prevents him from putting them down the usual way: using a 25-cent bullet for euthanasia instead of paying for my services on the less cherished dogs.

The old, tough, leathery-skinned farmers put on a tough persona during these visits. If you look past the tough exterior, their pain is easily observed. A few have tears flowing down their cheeks. Others try to hide their pain by being humorous with lame jokes. Farmers with quiet personalities often become more talkative and vice versa.

In my 30-year career to this point, I can never remember visiting euthanize a cat. The weird thing is that this unusual request came twice on the same day by two old farmers. One farmer had a favorite outdoor male cat with gigantic problems. The other had a favorite indoor female cat with equally enormous problems. The cats lived on different sides of the county, but I made both sites on one trip.

The first stop was at a long-term client's house to euthanize his favorite barn cat. Jim really loved this old mouser, so much so that when he moved, he moved the cat with him to his new barn. Rascal was an ancient barn cat, which was unusual. Barn cats have very limited life expectancies because of their hazardous lifestyles.

Rascal was a nappy-looking grey and white cat. He seldom groomed himself and didn't seem to care what he looked like. He cared even less about what other beings thought of his appearance. His appearance grew even rougher when he began battling teeth and mouth infections. His desire to groom himself diminished even more as he battled oral ulcers and kidney failure with age.

Jim fought back tears as I pulled into his driveway. We stumbled through an awkward conversation about the weather as I exited the car. I examined one of his other cats before we turned our attention to Rascal.

He was old, grumpy, and in pain. The ulcers prevented him from opening his mouth to eat without screaming in anguish. The pain was intense. He associated the pain with eating and stayed away from the food dish despite starving.

Jim had a dry sense of humor and usually enjoyed teasing me quite a bit. His teasing remarks were subdued on this day. He tried to brush off the lump in his throat and the tears in his eyes by claiming it was his wife who was having a tough time with the euthanasia. My technician and I could tell otherwise.

Because of his discomfort, it surprised me when Jim made a comment that I thought was a joke. "Hey Doc, would you mind burying Rascal for me?" Jim inquired, with a smile on his face.

I chuckled and thought he was kidding, as he is wont to do. I figured he was not wanting to dig a hole and was asking me to do it for him.

"I'm serious, Doc! I got the hole dug already and wanted you to just cover him up!"

I felt horrible. I assured him I would. I apologized and told him I thought he was joking with me to dig the hole.

I thought about how badly I had misread the conversation as I covered Rascal with the barn dirt that I'm sure he enjoyed pooping in days earlier. It embarrassed me. I had made an uncomfortable situation even more so.

More frustrating for me was the fact that I'd missed a golden opportunity to be perfect. I didn't ponder my mistake long because the weather was freezing; the wind was howling, and I wasn't wearing a coat.

Despite sticking my foot in my mouth, I think I may have regained some lost points when I returned to the garage with Jim's shovel. Tears were running down my face. Jim thought the tears resulted from sadness. Tears were indeed present, but they were mainly the result of freezing ocular tissue.

Take Half a Baby Aspirin and Call Me In the Morning

The most annoying emergency calls I receive are early Saturday or Sunday mornings, just after the beer joints close. Drunks get home about two in the morning and decide to call me about their sick animal. The story line is always the same.

"My old dog is gonna die unless you see him, and you need you to see him right now!"

The excessively high blood alcohol level removes all the caller's tact and respect for anyone else. They are often very aggressive and demanding. After struggling to get answers to a few simple questions, I find that the animal has been sick for about a week.

In addition, the drunks really don't want to spend any money. They've already spent it all on Jack Daniels. The good thing about being rude to these people is they will remember nothing the next morning.

This Saturday night the phone rang loudly about 11:30. It seemed much later to me because I was in a deep sleep. After slapping the alarm clock several times, I realized I needed to answer the phone instead of assaulting the alarm clock.

As I said hello, the sound of uncontrollable giggles met me coming from what sounded like a group of high school girls. The giggling caller tried to act mature as she yelled at her friends to be quiet several times. My ear rang from both the sound of the phone ringing loudly and the sound of a drunk juvenile screaming at her friends to shut up.

She yelled, "The vets gonna know we're having a party if ya'll don't shut up!"

This was obvious, and her command brought squeals and more giggles.

When the noise level diminished, the caller began, "Well, you see Mr., Ummm. I mean Dr, Vet, I had some friends over and, well ah, we, ah, had some grapes soaking in Everclear. You do know what Everclear is don't cha? We, anyway (more giggles). My dog ate some, and he is like, ah, stumbling around and staggering. Uh, ah, I think he's drunk and if my Mom's dog dies, she will kill me! What should I do?"

She slurred on and on without finding a stopping point. Every one of her words seemed to weigh a hundred pounds. The conversation was painstakingly slow.

I could finally determine the dog was a 7-pound Yorkie named Cooter. I was familiar with Cooter and had cared for him since he was a puppy. We guessed he had consumed about three grapes about an hour earlier.

Even though Cooter was staggering, stumbling and feeling no pain, he was responsive and awake. He did not bark during our conversation. If he had, I'll bet his bark would also have been slurred, heavy and loud.

Despite his small size, I was sure this would not be a toxic level of alcohol. After all, this was probably not the first time he had partied with the group, so a tolerance was already built. I made her promise to make sure Cooter ingested no more "party grapes". I also begged her to keep him from the beer bong.

She giggled and asked, "How did you know that we have one of those?"

Partying was not the actual use for drinking alcohol in pets. At that time, drinking alcohol was used to treat animals exposed to antifreeze. Antifreeze poisons animals by forming crystals in the animal's kidneys when it is metabolized. These crystals would then cause kidney failure. Alcohol binds to these anti-freeze metabolites and prevents crystals from forming. This saves the animal's kidneys and life.

Animals poisoned with antifreeze were given alcohol intravenously or by mouth over several days. This caused the antifreeze to be metabolized and removed by the liver instead of the kidneys. The alcohol was an effective treatment and saved many animals from suffering the slow, painful, horrible death of kidney failure.

I had been the bartender for many inebriated animals with this therapy and felt comfortable that Cooter's dose was well below the toxic levels. It would cause no problems, provided he didn't drive a car. With much conversation, I finally convinced the caller of this and hung up, hoping to return to a deep sleep.

Just as I dozed back to sleep, the phone rang again. I picked up the receiver and struggled to find my ear. I realized it was the same party on the other end. The noise level in the background had increased substantially. Because the fear of killing the dog was gone and the party grapes were kicking in, the girls appeared to be whooping it up.

Just as before, the girl tried to get her friends to pipe down so she could ask me a question. "My mom will be home in a few hours and I need to know how to sober up the dog. Do you have any suggestions?"

I suggested they hide him from her mother until the next day, so he could sleep it off. Through slurred speech, she wanted to know if she could force-feed him some black coffee like she was drinking. I told her to cool it down, make sure it was decaffeinated and go for it.

Cooter sure did not need to be hyped up on caffeine as well. Thankfully, this was the last call from the party girls, and I could once again slumber in peace.

Late the next day, I got a call from Cooter's mom. She explained she had been gone for several days and got home late last night. She was worried because Cooter was acting strangely. He did not greet her at the door when she got home, which was very unusual.

"Since I have been gone for several days, I do not know how long he has been acting this way. He looks like he has a terrible headache and doesn't feel well. He sure seems grumpy and loud noises really bother him," she explained.

"My daughter seems to feel the same way, and I wonder if they could have the same thing. Maybe a virus or something?"

As I listened to her story, I wrestled with the thoughts in my head as to the approach I should take. Should I fill her in and rat her daughter out or should I play dumb?

I stayed out of this mess. I played along and explained that there was a flu bug going around town in dogs that was causing headaches and body pain. It was a fast-acting virus which came and went quickly.

I assured her that humans could not get the dog disease, so her daughter was probably suffering from something else. I left the door open though and told her they could have consumed the same spoiled food or toxin and gotten sick at the same time.

I advised her to keep him in a calm, dark, quiet room and give him a small dose of baby aspirin to ease his pain. She probably got the same advice from her physician when she called and inquired about her daughter's hangover.

Divine Intervention

Bob was a retired Chief of Police. He was a bachelor who had lost his wife several years earlier to cancer. Bob was an elderly man facing the common struggles that plague older people. Standing and walking were a battle for him. While he didn't realize it, his close friends could tell his mental capabilities were also fading.

Bob's best friend and constant companion was a geriatric schnauzer named Sam. Bob and Sam spent every waking moment together. I often saw Sam and Bob driving around town, in my office for exams, and when Bob worked on my golf cart.

Every time I saw them, I had to make a conscious effort not to call them by the wrong name. I occasionally slipped and called them by the wrong name anyway. I would call Bob, Sam and Sam, Bob. Neither seemed to mind, and each responded as if I had called them the correct name.

Sam was a wonderful dog that battled several life-threatening problems through the years. He was prone to kidney infections, pancreatitis and getting wounds from neighborhood fights. Even though he didn't like me all that much, he was always cordial and tolerated my pokes, prods, and intrusions.

Bob cherished his long-term companion and pampered him. They were two old friends that looked after each other day in and day out. One could not be found without the other.

As they aged, they each suffered from severe arthritis and degenerative joint disease. Both Sam and Bob labored and grunted as they walked side by side to their destination. Watching the process made my joints hurt, and it was difficult to observe.

My compassionate office staff learned to watch for Bob when he pulled into the parking lot. They would run out to his car to get Sam for his grooming or other office appointments. The girls acted like Sonic carhops, and Bob even tipped them occasionally.

Besides being compassionate, the staff had another motive. It kept Bob's cigar smoke from making the office reek. Even during a brief visit, the smoke would fill the waiting room. Bob paid no attention to the No Smoking sign. He was from the era of when all real men smoked.

Sadly, as time passed, Sam had more and more struggles with his health and suffered a catastrophic illness and stroke. Bob and I had to make a pet owner's most difficult decision. Sam had been ill for a few weeks and a major stroke had made him incapacitated. It was time to put Sam to sleep and relieve his suffering.

While pet owners hate to decide on euthanasia for an old pet, I am thankful that we have that last favor we can grant a suffering friend. Even though it is the best decision, this process is very traumatic and difficult for pet owners. It is the only negative aspect of having a pet.

Bob was extremely emotional when he finally made this tough decision. His pain was deep and palpable as he sobbed in my office. His tears flowed as his yells echoed through the clinic. I was also very emotional because of his pain.

I often carry the events of the day's work home with me, and this sadness weighed on me that night. I knew the pain and loneliness that Bob must have felt at home without his long-term friend and companion. I worried that, because of losing his second-best friend, Bob's health might also deteriorate. He remained on my mind most of the next day as I worked through my busy schedule.

I administered first vaccinations to four new schnauzer puppies the next day. The pups were as cute as they come. They belonged to a client who never arrived promptly for her appointments. On some days, she just didn't show up at all.

Uncharacteristically, though, she showed up 10 minutes early for her appointment this day.

The pups were adorable and good-natured. There was one large black male pup that reminded me of Sam. I commented to the owner and my technician that Bob needed to see this pup but left it at that. I knew Bob would be nervous about getting a new pup because of the stresses of training a pup. Bob's arthritis and mental issues would make it difficult to manage and house-train a new pup.

I vaccinated all four dogs and sent them to the front desk while I filled out their charges. As I handed the ticket to my receptionist, she informed me that Bob was waiting to visit with me. It was remarkable timing. I arrived at the front desk just as Bob was admiring the puppies from a distance. He was very curious and wanted to see the pups, but only from a distance.

I greeted Bob and made the mistake of asking how he was doing. This inquiry caused him to break down and cry in front of all the people in the waiting room. As he cried, he and I made our way to a more private exam room.

Once he regained his composure, he informed me he was too lonely and wondered what I thought about the idea of him getting a new dog. We discussed how there would never be another Sam, but a new dog would have its own personality and make a good friend, eventually.

We also talked about his legitimate concern over house-training a new puppy. Bob's limited mobility made it difficult, and he didn't feel he was up for that challenge.

There was one breeder in town who would house-break a new dog for a fee, and she was the lady in the waiting room with the four schnauzer pups. Bob's eyes opened wide, and his spirits rose as he asked me to check with her to see if she would do that for him.

I exited the room and caught the breeder before she left. I discovered she was paying her bill slowly so that she might see Bob again, hoping to make a sale. It was a perfect match.

She visited with Bob and agreed to house-break the puppy. Bob wanted a male and the only male she had left was the large black pup that looked like Sam. The owner had mentioned earlier that she wanted to keep the black pup as a stud. Her mind changed when she witnessed Bob's sadness.

It was an immediate sell. In an unusual negotiation, the breeder asked Bob what he could afford to pay. She was worried about his financial capabilities and wanted him to have this pup. She did not know that Bob was a very wealthy man and could afford whatever it cost.

Bob said, "It doesn't matter, I can pay whatever it takes!"

He was determined to have that puppy and had more than adequate finances. The breeder stuttered a bit and ask for $400 for the pup. She had received much more for the littermates. Bob counter-offered to pay $500 and the deal was done.

Beau's training went well and quickly. He moved in with Bob a few short days later. His personality and attitude were much different, but he and Bob bonded well, and they became inseparable. Beau was laid-back and easygoing.

As Bob's health and mental faculties deteriorated, Beau didn't seem to care. He stretched out next to Bob as Bob sat naked with his leg propped up on the lawn chair outside in his front yard. Bob thought he was in the hot tub while Beau enjoyed a nap. The passing cars which honked at them only slightly annoyed both of them.

Beau's calm personality and demeanor were good for Bob's health. It was a match made in heaven. Beau was proud to stroll beside Bob as the pair walked down Main Street one afternoon, wearing nothing but a collar and a walking cane.

It is rare that we can recognize God's work and presence in our daily lives. I recognized this day that Divine Intervention had made all the events occur simultaneously and that this deal was predestined.

One In A Million Shot, Doc!

Veterinarians get many requests to do tasks we are not licensed to do or technically qualified to perform. Most of the requests are from friends or clients requesting medical services. Generally, the requests are an attempt to save money because they know we can't charge for the help.

Occasionally, the person really trusts and values your skills or diagnostic abilities. This is a tremendous compliment. Other times, it results from the veterinarian being the only medical professional for miles around.

My wife called me at the office late one afternoon because one of our close family friends had a dilemma. It seems Skyler, their kindergarten-age son, had a problem that the school nurse couldn't handle. The story was that while Skyler was lying down for a nap at school, a piece of tape he had been playing with fell directly into his ear canal.

He tried to remove it himself without success. It was deep in his ear and he could not get a grip on it.

Instead, he had actually stuffed it further down into his ear canal. Skyler was very uncomfortable. All the local physicians were booked solid and unable to see him until the next day. The school nurse tried to grab it with tweezers and flush it out with saline, but was unsuccessful in each effort.

Skyler arrived at my office with his head tilted to one side and was not his usual outgoing self. He resembled a large hunting dog with a tick in his ear. I placed him up on the dog-room exam table and made the usual jokes about giving him a rabies shot and threatening to muzzle him. He ignored my attempts at humor and hoped I was a better veterinarian than comedian.

I used the small-animal otoscope and went in for a gentle peak. Sure enough, there was a piece of tape rolled up tightly and lodged in his ear canal. The tape was long and right against his eardrum. It was scratching his ear drum and creating a great deal of discomfort.

I used the right-angled forceps to pull out the wad of tape. Skyler's mother was delighted. However, Skylar did not share her enthusiasm and still seemed a little uncomfortable. I went back in to take another look.

After entering the ear canal once again, the reason for his discomfort was obvious. Resting near his ear drum was a second rolled-up piece of tape that was larger than the first. I grasp the tape with the forceps and tugged the tape out as Skyler screamed. He felt better immediately until the questions from his mother began.

Skyler's mother pressed him with the obvious questions. It might be believable that a single piece of tape fell into the ear. It would be a one in a hundred million chance for a second piece to accidentally fall into the ear at the same time.

Skyler was the typical male and tried to stick with his story. He eventually cracked like a nut when his mother increased the pressure.

"Well, ah, ah, ah, ah, ya' see ah, Mom," he stammered. "Mrs. Rutz had noticed that a few pieces of tape had been pulled off her bulletin board and she was really angry. She said if she found out who was doing it, she would send them to the office for swats! I had two pieces of tape on my desk that the guy next to me had pulled off the bulletin board and I panicked!"

Also, like the typical male, he tried to diffuse the blame by accusing his unnamed neighbor.

"I crammed the tape into my ears to keep her from seeing them. After recess, they began to hurt really bad and I couldn't get 'em out." He finished his story with tears in his eyes.

Skyler's parental punishment was mild compared to amount of his suffering all day with the tape poking his ear drum. It's good though that he learned this valuable lesson so early in his school life: it's much better to swallow small, non-metal, non-sharp objects rather than stuff them into other body orifices to avoid detection. That is a valuable lesson for all males, no matter their age.

That's A Crappy Smile

Some people share too much personal information with total strangers. They seem to lack the gene responsible for preventing over-sharing of private information. As my years of dealing with the public go by, I am rarely surprised by what people say or do. The information they share either makes your eyes water, makes your mouth drop open, makes you laugh, makes you gag or all the above.

Mrs. Hopkins was a large woman who talked nonstop. Most of the time, she was well into another story by the time she realized what question you had just ask. She would change directions and answer your question before returning to her story.

These stories always involved more personal information than I cared to learn. Even though she only wanted the bare minimum done to her pet with each visit, her appointments lasted a long time because of her ramblings. I could have already retired if I had charged her by the word.

She called the clinic one day to ask me a couple of quick questions. I had never spoken with her on the phone, but I was sure that it would not be quick. I knew it would take a very long time to answer her two quick questions. She began a convoluted journey to her first question.

"Well Doc, you see I lost a tooth out of my bridge. Do you have a bridge? This bridge has never really fit right and gives me constant problems. It clicks and pops and just won't stay in. I started to take it back to the dentist, but I haven't had the chance. They are so busy that they never have time to see me anyway. They just rush me in and out without listening to me."

She continued without taking a breath. "One tooth on the bridge has been wiggly. The tooth had been loose for a while, and it finally fell out. When it fell onto the carpet, my little dog Furby, you do remember Furby? He is the 3-pound Chihuahua pup that I bring in. He is brown and white, small and just adorable.

"But I'll bet you see a lot of adorable puppies. Have you seen many today? Well, anyway, when that tooth fell out, Furby snatched it up and ate it! First of all, will it hurt him?"

The story wore me plumb out. I spent most of it wondering what techniques the dentist used to speed her out of the office. I was glad to get a word in edge-wise and seized the moment of silence to answer.

"The tooth should not hurt Furby at all," I answered as she started her next monologue.

"Oh, that is great news!" she exclaimed. "Now, for the second question, how long do you think it will take for him to pass the tooth?"

I informed her it may take a few days to pass, but it would eventually make its way out. Most conversations with genetically normal people would end here. This one continued and took an immediate turn for the worse.

"I told my husband that if he watched the dog take a dump and saw the tooth that I would do all the dirty work. I'd dig the tooth out of the turd, clean it up and put it back on my bridge. I went to the Chinese food restaurant and got some chop sticks.

"I figure those will be a great tool to dig the tooth out of that slimy turd. That tooth is expensive, and I can't pay $125 for a new one! I know it sounds gross, but how bad can it be?"

She wondered aloud about how to best clean the tooth. I chuckled and gagged at the same time. I offered no help, but it did not matter because she went on to another story. At the next moment of silence, I wished her the best of luck and told her to keep me posted on the progress.

As soon as I hung up the phone, I texted the local physician to give him a heads-up. I warned him that her husband might come into his office with the complaint of "my wife's breath smelled like crap." I advised him to check between the teeth of the bridge for fecal remnants before running a battery of tests.

Mrs. Hopkins came into the office a week later for Furby's last set of puppy vaccinations. I looked at her while she rambled nonstop to see if she had the tooth in place. She had not yet found the tooth and still had a gaping hole between her upper front teeth.

The large hole made her whistle slightly as she spoke. She sounded a bit like Donald Duck talking at warp speed. When I ask about the tooth, she kept running her tongue in and out of the toothless gap, without missing a word.

She sputtered, "I looked and looked for that tooth. I even took those chop sticks and dissected the poop piles carefully. I went through them with a fine-tooth comb with no luck!

"I had to follow the dang dog at night because my husband wouldn't follow him with a flashlight to see where he dropped a deuce. He was afraid the neighbors would make fun of him. It was tough because Furby does not like to poop with a spotlight shining on him and it took a very long time."

It was too bad she couldn't find the tooth. The brown stained tooth would have made a great conversation piece. Mrs. Hopkins could have gone around showing everyone her crap-eating grin. It's for the better though. Her food would have tasted like crap regardless of how thoroughly she cleaned the tooth.

On the other hand, it would have given her a good excuse for her constant chattering and diarrhea of the mouth. She would have a reason for having a potty mouth if she felt the need to swear like a sailor.

The story has a happy ending. Several kind-hearted people at the bank that always covered her hot checks pooled their money together and bought her a new bridge. The thought of seeing and smelling the poop tooth every day tugged at their hearts and purse strings.

Irony

Benny is one of my favorite clients. He's the sort of guy that is fun to be around and always has marvellous stories. He is a wealthy cattle producer with houses in several communities. Benny's talented and had developed his own genetically unique, registered breed of cattle.

His mind is well developed, and he thinks outside the box. Benny is never afraid to try something new and is often the first to do so. In his younger days, he loved to have a good time and was never too far away from a party. He lived, worked and played very hard.

Whiskey was his beverage of choice when he was young. He told me he drank early and often while smoking like a chimney. Benny would disappear from town for months and then return like a whirlwind.

Benny was thin and wiry, just like most of his animals. His cattle were thin but very productive, with little maintenance required. Unlike most cowboys, he pampered his house cat and two fearless dachshunds.

The two dachshunds take after Benny. They chase and harass the cattle while nipping at the enormous beast's hind legs. The occasional kick to the chin or stumble and crash doesn't curb their enthusiasm. They are like little SCUD missiles.

The cat was different. He was extremely independent and didn't give a rat's behind about what you thought or how he looked. Benny did not strike me as a cat person, which intrigued me because he particularly loved this cat. After I had treated the cat for years, Benny shared a story and I found out why he loved it so.

There was a time when the drinking and partying almost ended Benny's life. The gallons of Jack Daniels whiskey were damaging his liver. The constant smoking was damaging his lungs. He was a wreck.

As is often the case, the need for Benny to stop his destructive behavior hit him hard and fast. He recalled finding himself in the hospital, trying to get his demons under control. His liver was damaged almost beyond the point of repair, and he had an awakening.

The recovery process involved Alcoholics Anonymous meetings and going through the program to recovery. He was so strong-willed that once he decided it needed to be done, he never looked back. Benny recollected to me that the battle was long and painful, but he would say that it was well worth the result.

It had been a long time since I had seen his cat named JD. As soon as I walked into the room, I could see that he was extremely ill, and the result was probably not going to be good.

The physical exam revealed a very thin cat with a small liver and yellow skin. The jaundice and small liver indicated poor liver function. Laboratory tests confirmed my suspicions. The liver was scarred and not working well. The cirrhosis of the liver was preventing it from doing its vital function. JD was in a state of advanced liver failure.

Unlike in the human world, liver cirrhosis in animals is not caused by alcohol consumption. It can be caused by many infections, metabolic processes, or toxins. The result is generally the same and not good.

Treatment success is limited because the original cause of the liver damage has occurred several weeks before presentation for therapy. Once the liver has scarred to this level, there is little that can be done.

The news was hard for Benny. He had pampered this cat for years and it had a special meaning to him. He rescued the stray cat soon after being released from the hospital and beginning his sobriety. The cat's name of JD stood for Jack Daniels.

The cat became his substitute for whiskey. Nurturing the small helpless kitten became his focus and helped him overcome his addiction. It's ironic that the cat which had helped prevent him from dying of cirrhosis of the liver was now dying of the same disease.

JD was buried along with a full bottle of his namesake on the ranch. His ultimate resting place is just outside his favorite window next to the house he patrolled for years. The buried bottle was the only bottle that Benny had purchased in 17 years.

Don't Laugh – It Could Happen to You

The most challenging part of being a veterinarian is dealing with the people and not the animals. The feelings and responses of people are very unpredictable and difficult to read.

It amazes my staff and I at the high level of grumpiness in some people and the constant state of happiness in others. Some people find the bad in any situation, while others find a bright spot in the same situation. While I have a tendency to be grumpy, I yearn to be more optimistic and positive.

Martha is not a tough person to read. Her emotions are close to the surface and easy to detect. She is an elderly woman who was usually bubbly and talkative.

Since her latest husband died, she has enjoyed traveling to attend Bluegrass Festivals all over the country. She dresses very young for her age in cowgirl clothing. Martha loves turquoise and jewelry, which in the Bluegrass world is a natural mix. She talks quickly and constantly without waiting for answers to her questions.

Martha had a Schnauzer named Blue Shadow that was often ill, especially in her older years. Blue Shadow was prone to having an inflamed pancreas, as many old Schnauzers are, and needed to be on a strict diet. Since Martha was slipping in her old age and was very forgetful, she would often feed Shadow the wrong food.

About every two weeks, we would treat Shadow for vomiting and diarrhea. I explained Shadow's dietary needs every time Martha came in, but with limited success. She rambled on so fast that she couldn't hear me, even if she could remember it. Martha's rambling often included odd stories and humorous comments, which kept me laughing.

Several years ago, Martha came in to get Shadow's digestive tract straightened out and was in rare form. She immediately went into her rapid-fire talking and storytelling as soon as I entered the exam room. She talked about her latest husband named Harold.

"I just don't know what I'm going to do with myself, Randy," she began in her cheerful voice. "When you get old, things just start to wear out. I can't hear anything or remember anything anymore. It's just terrible!

"A while back, Harold's chest and back hurt so bad he couldn't sleep in bed. I left him on the couch where he was more comfortable and went on to bed. I tried and tried to get him to go to see Dr. Siewert for his pain, but he was so stubborn and tough, he wouldn't go. He got to where he could only sleep on the couch night after night."

I couldn't help but to think at this point that it may have just been to get away from her constant chatter.

"One late night," she continued, "I couldn't sleep due to all the moaning and racket he was making in the living room. He was carrying on like a mad man. 'Ohhh... OOhhh... OOOhhh... help... Help... HELP!' he yelled and wouldn't be quiet.

"I was so mad! I finally went in to tell him to be quiet because I couldn't sleep. I told him he was so noisy that I couldn't get a bit of rest and would be too tired to go to the upcoming Bluegrass concert. Through his moaning and groaning, he said, 'Honey, I'm sick and need you to call the ambulance'. He had rolled off the couch and was laying on the living room floor all hunkered up."

She continued on with no signs of the impending bad news, "He was such a big man, and I am so small I couldn't budge him. I had to leave him there in that odd position 'cause I could not roll him over. I knew it had to be bad because he never wanted to go the doctor. I went back to my room to call the ambulance.

"On my way back to get the phone, I looked at myself in the mirror and said, 'Self, you can't go to the hospital looking like that!' I had to agree with myself because I looked rough and knew I couldn't be seen looking like I was, so I went to the bedroom to put on some clothes before I called.

"You know, it takes a while for a lady to get ready. I combed my hair and put on some make-up. Not a lot but just enough to look presentable. I sat down on the bed to pull on my boots and, Randy, you won't believe this, but I fell right back to sleep and never called the ambulance!"

I struggled to keep my laughter under control, but the last comment did the trick, and I let it rip. My technician was also laughing.

Martha's mood changed dramatically. She became angry and scolded me, "Well, it's not funny, Randy. When I finally woke up the next morning at 8 am, Harold was dead! He had a heart attack and died in the night. I felt soooo bad, but I was just soooo tired and I didn't know he was that sick."

My laughter turned into a dropped jaw. She told this story like it was no big deal and it could happen to anybody. I pictured poor Harold laying on the living room floor, grasping to hold on to life just a few minutes longer while anticipating the ambulance's arrival any minute.

Despite the bombshell she had just dropped, Martha didn't give us a long time to ponder this story. The sternness in her voice escaped as she went right into telling me about her next Bluegrass Festival trip and how she could listen for hours to that lively music.

In the back of my mind, I couldn't help but think poor old Harold would still be alive if his moans and groans had sounded more like a whining Bluegrass singer instead of the desperate cries of a dying man. He might also still be alive if Martha had chosen a sensible slip-on shoe rather than hard to manage cowboy boots.

Mother-In-Love

Edna was a sweet, loving grandmother who had a lot of spunk. She had a constant companion in her old age. Her 2-pound Maltese basically lived in her purse. She carried the pampered pet with her everywhere she went.

Rice was equally spunky and traveled tucked inside Edna's huge purse without making a sound. He sat through hours and hours of doctor visits and eye exams without so much as a whimper. No one ever knew he was stowed away in her luggage-sized handbag.

Edna loved Rice and took good care of him because he was her constant companion. They have identical personalities. Edna enjoyed giving me a hard time when I gave Rice an injection. The insults really crossed the line if I ever had to take his rectal temperature. Rice had a difficult time as a puppy, so I got verbally abused often when he was young.

On one exam, Edna seemed troubled and less ornery than usual. She seemed much more subdued. When I asked if she was feeling okay, she broke down and shared with me what was troubling her.

"I suffered through a long, difficult night last night. You see, I lost my dear husband several years ago to heart disease and last Saturday I finally broke down and sold his lawn mower. It was his pride and joy. Since it has been five years since he passed, and I don't mow the lawn myself anymore, I decided to get rid of it. That was very traumatic for me since he dearly loved that silly mower".

Edna was visibly shaken, and tears filled her eyes as she continued her story. "Well, last night, my husband's spirit visited me in my dream. I was so glad to see him! He seemed preoccupied and was very antsy. He insisted on mowing the lawn!

"I kept pleading with him to sit down and talk because we had so much to get caught up on. I wanted to introduce him to Rice and ask him all about heaven. He would not listen to any of it. Instead, he hurried to the garage to get his mower. When he got there and discovered that I had sold his lawn mower, he was beyond angry! I cried and tried to express to him my torment and anguish in making that decision, but he was unforgiving!"

At this point, everyone in the room had tears in their eyes as we shared in her torment and anguish. It was a sad event, and I struggled to find the words to comfort her. As I stuttered and stammered around trying to say the right thing, Edna's demeanor changed abruptly. Her next comment contained a glimmer of hope for her and entirely changed the mood in the room.

She giggled with delight and said, "Well, you know, it's not all bad. I feel much better since I've learned you can torment someone from beyond the grave. At least now I know I'll be able to make my son-in-law's life a living hell for years after I'm gone. So, I've got that going for me."

About the Author

Dr. Skaggs' roots are in a small town in Texas. For as long as he can remember, he loved animals and made it his mission to become an animal doctor. His goal is to make every dog's tail wag, every kitten purr, and every horse and cow buck and play in the fields. He began jotting down unique experiences occurring with animals and owners and has been doing it for thirty years. As a country vet, his practice hasn't been specialized or limited to dogs, cats, birds, exotic animals, or livestock. His clinic takes whatever patients walk in the door and he never knows what that might include. The work can be messy, is often loud, sometimes dangerous and often humorous.

Note From the Author

Word-of-mouth is crucial for any author to succeed. If you enjoyed *Country Vet*, please leave a review online—anywhere you are able. Even if it's just a sentence or two. It would make all the difference and would be very much appreciated.

Thanks!
Randy L. Skaggs, DVM

We hope you enjoyed reading this title from:

BLACK ROSE writing™

www.blackrosewriting.com

Subscribe to our mailing list—*The Rosevine*—and receive **FREE** books, daily deals, and stay current with news about upcoming releases and our hottest authors.

Scan the QR code below to sign up.

Already a subscriber? Please accept a sincere thank you for being a fan of Black Rose Writing authors.

View other Black Rose Writing titles at www.blackrosewriting.com/books and use promo code **PRINT** to receive a **20% discount** when purchasing.

www.ingramcontent.com/pod-product-compliance
Lightning Source LLC
Chambersburg PA
CBHW072007070526
44583CB00015B/1374